# DOWN IN BRISTOL BAY

ALSO BY BOB DURR

*Poetic Vision and the Psychedelic Experience*
*On the Mystical Poetry of Henry Vaughan*

❀

# DOWN IN

# BRISTOL BAY

*High Tides, Hangovers, and Harrowing
Experiences on Alaska's Last Frontier*

B O B   D U R R

THOMAS
DUNNE
BOOKS

ST. MARTIN'S PRESS ≈ NEW YORK

THOMAS DUNNE BOOKS.
An imprint of St. Martin's Press.

Library of Congress Cataloging-in-Publication Data

Durr, R. A.
    Down in Bristol Bay / high tides, hangovers, and harrowing
experiences on Alaska's last frontier / Robert Durr, — 1st ed.
        p.      cm.
    ISBN 0-312-20529-5
    "Thomas Dunne books."
    1. Bristol Bay Region (Alaska)—Social life and customs.
2. Frontier and pioneer life—Alaska—Bristol Bay Region.   3. Durr,
R. A.   4. Bristol Bay Region (Alaska) Biography.   5. Fishers—
Alaska—Bristol Bay Region Biography.   I. Title.
F912.B74D87    1999
979.8'4—dc21
[B]                                                                    99-21748
                                                                           CIP

First Edition: June 1999

10   9   8   7   6   5   4   3   2   1

*To my family, with love,*
*and to the wild woods and waters,*
*in gratitude*

# CONTENTS

*Acknowledgments*    *ix*

*Introduction*    *xi*

Prologue: The Ballad of Bristol Bay    1

1   Getting There: Phase 1    3

2   Getting There: Phase 2    36

3   Our First Season Fishing    65

4   Our First Big Run, '65    92

5   The Day the Boat Went Down and Only One
Survived    110

6   High Boat    125

7   Two Days of the Love-in Girl    138

8   Fiasco, or What Became of *Port N Storm*    158

9   A Night on the Outside    164

10   Threading the Needle    181

11   Party    188

*Epilogue*    *218*

## ACKNOWLEDGMENTS

The making of a book is like the making of a life: So many people, places, and events go into the mix it's impossible to name them all. The writer can acknowledge only those close at hand and directly involved in the production of his work. For me, first and foremost, must be the Great Land itself, Alaska's wild places, the backcountry, especially Bristol Bay and this little lake in the Susitna Valley that has been home for almost thirty years. The spirit of this place and this life in the woods have been formative for me as a man and writer in more ways than I can know or say.

But had it not been for the support of my family, most importantly my former wife, Carol, I would not have been able to break away from academia and suburban life to come to Alaska in the first place. Carol was an unswerving mate, and she became an extraordinary wilderness woman, with the kind of mettle it takes to handle the often severe challenges of frontier life. She could have nipped my venture in the bud, but she did not, and I'm grateful to her for that and, of course, for so much more.

My sons, Steve and Jon, and my daughters, Sarah and Beth,

in the course of many conversations over the years, helped me decide what kind of book this should be. Their unremitting insistence that this ex-professor must refrain from lecturing and get on with the story no doubt saved my book from swamping in the tide rips of philosophizing. Steve, my oldest son, shared many of my Bristol Bay experiences with me and has been invaluable in setting straight my recollections. He also came up with the subtitle for the book and has been my closest critic and adviser through all the drafts.

It's a pleasure to express my thanks to Jane Dystel, my agent, for her heartening enthusiasm about the manuscript and for her expert help in all matters pertaining to publication; to my editor at St. Martin's, Pete Wolverton, for his careful and sensitive critique, which resulted in many improvements, large and small, and for being a great guy to work with; and to Sue Llewellyn, my copy editor, who went through the manuscript with a finetooth comb, culling out the inevitable typos, misspellings, and the like, as well as questioning various points of style and suggesting alternatives, many of which I was happy to accept.

I owe a welcome debt of gratitude to my friend Charlotte Arrington, who not only did a most professional job of typing the final draft and dealing with all the insertions, deletions, and compositional changes over a period of months, but who also brought her editing experience to bear upon many matters of consequence in the writing and formatting of the manuscript.

Finally, last but certainly not least, there are Gene Pope and D Inn Crowd. They didn't teach me how to be a good fisherman, but they did teach me how to cut loose. To them I say, "Carry on, but whatever it is don't drop it." They live in my memory always with a smile, bully lads all.

Talkeetna, Alaska
Winter, 1998–1999

The frontier has always been a peculiarly American obsession. In the early days it meant the possibility of a new start: If you were down on your luck and hard-pressed, you could leave the established world behind and head west into the unknown. But it was more than that, too, more than escape from pinched economic circumstances or social disadvantages. Its lure could operate on another level of consciousness as well. If you felt the parlors of civilization to be too stuffy or effete, too many rules and regulations, too tight a constriction of something inside you that wasn't born to be ruled, you could turn away and scent the air of freedom blowing in from the mountains and prairies, where the only law was nature. The mere fact of the frontier, that it existed, fostered a rebellious, adventurous spirit among the people: There was a way out. To this day, a certain aspect of the American posture of independence reflects the historic fact of the frontier. We have never put it behind us. In countless books, magazines, movies, and TV dramas the frontiersman and the cowboy live on, amalgams of fact and fiction, figures of mythic proportions, represented by an unbroken line of heroes from Daniel Boone and Natty Bumpo to the prototypical westerner portrayed by actors like John Wayne and Gary Cooper. Someone once remarked that in his secret heart every

American fancies himself a cowboy or pioneer, and I think that's true. The frontier and the Wild West have been the tireless dream of our collective imagination, unrolling before us in the theater of our longings.

The cause of this endless fascination is not Hollywood or Madison Avenue, whose renditions have often been so arbitrary, stereotyped, and ridiculous as to be repellent. The cause is in our genetic inheritance. For millions of years as hunter-gatherers we had lived every day as adventurers on the frontiers of the natural world. For millions of years we had been a free, wild, natural people. It was only a brief ten thousand years ago that we began to settle down to the accumulation of possessions and anxieties in towns and cities: not long enough, on the scale of evolutionary time, to turn us wholly into civilized creatures. Some part of us still yearns for the old freedoms. In odd moments apart, we can still hear the call of the wild.

❖

When I was growing up in Brooklyn, the West as frontier was long gone. All the land to the west coast had been settled and tamed. But there remained an amorphous territory that was still wild. Somewhere north or northwest was a vast land of forest and tundra stretching to the pole, where bears, wolves, moose, and caribou lived unconstrained, and only a handful of people— trappers, traders, miners, Indians, and Eskimo—roamed the immense expanse. The Wild West was gone, but the north woods were still there, in the real world. So there was one frontier left. For Americans, Alaska, the last frontier.

This book tells the story of how I went there during the sixties, a professor of English at Syracuse University desperate to get out of the world of words and into the wilderness, to start a new life on the solid footing of elemental existence. My wife and kids understood and supported me; but I knew I couldn't just drop us all into the woods and start living off the land—

not even the Native Americans could do that anymore. I needed to find a compatible way to earn some dollars, and I hit upon commercial salmon fishing as that way: If the northland was still wild, so was the sea.

The turn of events led me to an enormous and remote region of Alaska called Bristol Bay. Before I knew much about it—not even where it was situated in relation to the rest of the state—the name itself and the few impressions I had picked up about it conjured up images of steely seas and barren tundra swept by storms, a vague but provocative sense of place that lingered in my mind with a strange persistence, as though that stark land and the restless seas bordering it signified something beyond themselves, some essence or spirit still alive beneath the surface of modern life.

Far removed from the network of highways and roads in southcentral Alaska, Bristol Bay even now can be reached only by boat or airplane. It is sparsely settled, mainly by the indigenous peoples who have always lived there—Yup'ik Eskimo, Inuit, Aleuts, Athabascan Indians. Whites are still in the minority there, except perhaps in Dillingham, the regional population center, though of course their culture and technology are everywhere apparent. Salmon fishing was and still is the area's principal enterprise. It was salmon fishing that brought me to Bristol Bay in the summer of 1964, and it was in connection with salmon fishing that Gene Pope strode into my life.

When I first saw him coming toward me in the dusk, along the isolated gravel beach, his black hair whipping forward and his ragged jacket snapping in the wind off Iliamna Lake, I had the sensation (before I formed the thought) that in this man wilderness had assumed human shape. I saw flitting about his handsome, clean-cut features something irrepressible and possibly ruthless, a barely contained and altogether undomesticated energy and gusto. In him I thought I saw, alive and in person, the real thing: the authentic frontiersman. By then I had met other Alaskans, tough, capable men, rugged individualists in the

American way. I was partners with a man, Les VanDevere, who was himself all of that. But Gene Pope was something more, or something else.

Maybe Pope was in a sense no more than what I had imagined. Maybe I had carried the mold for him in my head and had fitted him into it. But there were dimensions to the man that could not have been prefigured, that only the light of experience could have revealed. Much of this portrait of a modern frontier turns on him and the friendship that grew between us: Pope and the Professor, as they came to call us, the wild man and the intellectual who would be wild.

●

The story I tell here is of adventures and dangers and also, often simultaneously, of misadventures and follies—occasionally of burlesque proportions—on land as well as at sea. The story unfolds episodically, somewhat like a series of scenes in a movie, in generally chronological order. But the suspense of a question underlies the episodes. I needed to prove up as a fisherman because I saw it as the best way to earn a living consistent with my overriding wish to live in the woods. Becoming a fisherman was the necessary first step, but there were imposing obstacles in the way. I knew nothing about the fisherman's trade, nothing about fish boats or drift nets, engines or hydraulic rollers, and next to nothing about the sea, about sandbars or tide rips, thirty-foot waves or twenty-foot tides. I was eager to learn, risks notwithstanding, but as luck or karma would have it, the companions I fell in with, notably Gene Pope and his pals, known as D Inn Crowd, were more interested in showing me how to drink than how to fish. As a result I learned the fisherman's trade haphazardly if at all, though I quickly became adept (even indispensable) at partying. And curiously, that untoward talent for carousing turned out to be a crucial factor, because for the fishermen—in my crowd mostly Native Alaskans (full bloods, half bloods, quarter bloods, hotbloods)—to accept me as one of their own and not just another white man after their fish, I had to emerge in their eyes an hombre, a man capable of going all the way in whatever direction booze or the winds of circumstance might take us, unfettered by concerns about decorum, money, or survival. Questions of health or morality aside, that's how it was.

"If you don't drink," said Louie Hereshka that first season, scowling at me, "you're no good."

I was easily convinced. Tired of the polite world of nervous egos, I was ready to be good on their terms. The question was, did I have the right kind of the wrong stuff to be one of them—one of D Inn Crowd, a bona fide Bristol Bay fisherman?

In Wildness is the preservation of the World. . . . Give me for my friends
and neighbors wild men, not tame ones.

— *T h o r e a u*


Given the nature of life, there may be no security, but only adventure.

— *R a c h e l   N a o m i   R e m e n*

# DOWN IN BRISTOL BAY

# PROLOGUE

## THE BALLAD OF BRISTOL BAY*
### Bob Durr

Come you sailors and you fishermen and listen to my song
I'll sing it to you right, but you might think it's wrong
May make you mad, but it's true what I say
It's all about the fellows down in Bristol Bay

Hard times on the water, down in Bristol Bay

Well, you run down to Bristol Bay
Gonna catch a lot of fish, make a big payday
I come around to see you and it's flip and flop
You're in hock to the cannery for everything you've got

Hard times on the water, down in Bristol Bay

The fishing's hot at Naknek, I heard it today
Gas her up and head her out of Nushagak Bay
You meet a bunch of boats a-coming back the other way
They say the nets are all smoking back in Nushagak Bay

Hard times on the water, down in Bristol Bay

Come the Fourth of July and the Big Run is here
Open up a jug and a case of beer

*Sung to the folk tune "Down on Penny's Farm," a sharecroppers' song.

1

*Sit on the beach, boys, and take your ease*
*Fish and Game needs escapement for the Japanese*

*Hard times on the water, down in Bristol Bay*

*Fishermen are sober down in Bristol Bay*
*High boat or average got no time to play*
*You open up a jug and ol' P. G.'ll say—*
*"You got smashed last night: no advance today"*

*Hard times on the water, down in Bristol Bay*

*The Bristol Bay fellows like to hang around bars*
*Some'll get you fish, and some'll get you scars*
*Both are kind of rough, and both are kind of wet*
*If you're looking for trouble, either one's a good bet*

*Hard times on the water, down in Bristol Bay*

*1*

## GETTING THERE: PHASE 1

The restiveness that underlay my days for so many years before I made my move to Alaska had no obvious origin in the circumstances of my life. At forty-three I was still fairly young, in good health, well married, with four bright and happy kids. My job as a professor of English at Syracuse University was respectable, tenured, and moderately well paid, with lots of time off, and I was considered a good teacher and scholar, liked by my students and colleagues. But many men and women have enjoyed these kinds of advantageous circumstances, which our society considers reason enough to be content, and yet have not been content. We learn of their nervous breakdowns or suicides with disbelief and dismay. Someone like Howard Hughes or Ernest Hemingway might come to mind.

If the conventional wisdom of our culture can be so wrong so often about the ingredients of contentment, and if your survey of your own life uncovers most of those ingredients in adequate measure and still you know that something is wrong, that you are not content but obscurely yearning, behind all the easy day-to-day facades, for some unknown factor, some imponderable missing quality of life, you will eventually refuse to run with the pack after the accepted goods of the world. And should it happen then that you come upon one or another of the authentic expressions of the ancient and universal wisdom of our species, the perennial philosophy—the teachings of Jesus and the Christian mystics, say, or of Siddhārtha Gautama or Lao-tzu or the Zen patriarchs, or perhaps a poet like Thomas Traherne or William Blake or Walt Whitman—you will be irresistibly drawn in search of the missing ingredient, the philosopher's stone that will transform your leaden life into imperishable gold. You will, perhaps without realizing it, start upon a singular quest. In my own case all the signs pointed to wilderness and a life reduced to elementals. I wanted to set my feet on bedrock again, to wriggle down through high-sounding ideas and enticing images onto the solid ground of mere existence, the fundamentals of human life. I wanted to come as close as I could to the life of "primitive" man, the original people. So, on summer vacations, while my colleagues toured Europe to savor history and culture, I traveled north and then northwest into prehistory and the aboriginal in search of the straight and narrow passage "to more than India," in Whitman's words, "to realms of primal thought and innocent intuition."

At first I headed blindly north into Canada, driving as far into the bush as the gravel and dirt roads could take me, camping along the way with my son Steve, who was then about ten years old. But northern Quebec and Ontario were predominantly flat, bushy: The country didn't appeal to me, I had no positive feeling for it. And I could see no way in those provinces that I could live in the woods and still earn the few necessary dollars. At home, when heated to the subject, I might rant and rave about finding a cave for us to live in, subsisting on nothing but birch bark and berries, but in actuality I knew we would need some cash income to make it.

In the third summer of exploration I took my whole family, in a Jeep station wagon with a rack on top loaded with camping gear, all the way across the continent to British Columbia. There, as far west as I could go, I again followed whatever dirt road there was leading away into the backcountry. Though the

land was magnificent, a wild, high terrain, not only did it promise to be difficult and costly to get a little piece of it to settle
on, but once more I could see no way to earn the necessary
dollars. Finally, in the summer of 1963 we traveled the rest of
the way north to Alaska: We were Americans, and maybe it
would be easier in the Great Land to find a way.

One day in that summer of 1963, while driving down the
Kenai Peninsula toward Homer, I stopped at a scenic bluff overlooking Cook Inlet, and we all piled out of the Jeep. The
younger kids ran about, glad to be released. While my wife,
Carol, watched them, Steve and I stood looking out across the
inlet. It was a brilliant windy day, the sky swept pale blue, and
cool for July by our New York standards, even though at the
same time the northern sun struck us as peculiarly intense, as if
its rays passed through the thin atmosphere without resistance,
or as if the atmosphere couldn't resist its power, so much fiercer
than the mild sun of New York skies.

Cook Inlet in actuality didn't correspond at all with the small
wedge of blue it had appeared to be on the maps I had studied
on the dining-room table of my house in New York State. The
inlet was a very big body of water, stretching away infinitely
south and across into the distance, where the pale mountains
on the far side seemed suspended in a sunlit haze above the
land.

Just below us a small boat, light gray and white, slowly made
its way against wind and wave. In the distance the inlet seemed
merely to be sparkling with whitecaps, but closer up, where that
little boat was, the waves looked big and dangerous. The boat
lurched, pounded, and rolled, periodically disappearing in spray.
Nets were coiled in the stern: a fish boat. It came to me in a
rush that there—down there with that boat crashing through
the waves—was the missing piece to complete my idea of the
good life, linking it to the pragmatics of making a living. Commercial salmon fishing could be the way to make it out of the
world of words and back to earth. How I was to become a fish-

erman I had as yet no idea, but I was sure it could be done. That a way was to present itself out of the blue within the next couple of days would have seemed to me at the time most unlikely, and that it happened seems to me now what—in a religious context—would have to be called providential.

❀

We drove on down to Homer, once more to the end of the road, and pitched camp on Homer Spit, the sandy finger of land extending from town and pointing across Kachemak Bay. The campground was only roughly developed, a dozen or so random clearings with fireplaces among the scrub spruce and willows. A man named Les VanDevere and his wife, Betty, and small son, Dyer, had pitched their wall tent in the clearing nearest ours. They had driven down from Kenai to do a little crabbing, and we got acquainted in the casual way of families sharing a campground.

Les had fled New Jersey and a mechanic's job ten years earlier. The boss had called him into the office one Friday afternoon. He had good news: Les could work right through the weekend. But Les failed to experience the expected elation at the prospect of overtime. He had made plans to go deer hunting. He decided on the spot that he would rather have the deer than the dollars, even if he didn't get the deer. He quit, sold his possessions, and headed north to Alaska. Now he made his living fishing for salmon in Cook Inlet, and I could tell from the way he held himself and cocked his cap that it had been the right move for him.

Before two nights had passed around the campfire, we had made plans for me to fly up alone the following summer to fish with him—but not in Cook Inlet.

"Bristol Bay," he said, glancing at me from behind his thick glasses with a curious sort of mocking smile, like a man who knew something he was sure I would want to know. He took another swallow from the whiskey bottle, which he called a jug. "If you're really after salmon, Bristol Bay is where you want to be." He paused, as though he had said everything that needed to be said. I waited. When I came to know him better, I realized he had been uncharacteristically talkative that night, thanks partly no doubt to the company of Jim Beam but also because we had started making plans and he was warming up to Bristol Bay. He poked at the fire with a stick. "I've wanted to get over there myself in the worst way for years now," he went on in the introverted voice of a private utterance, as though he were thinking out loud. "That's the big time in salmon fishing, over there." He glanced at me with a grin coming to his face. "Christ! In a good year the runs are so thick with fish you don't even need a net. You just lean over the side and shovel them on board!" He laughed explosively, as habitually silent men often do, as if the laugh had to force its way out through little-used channels under backed-up pressure.

VanDevere was tall and slim, along Gary Cooper or Jimmy Stewart lines, with a clean sweep to his jaw. He was silent again, leaning forward now, gazing into the fire, with his elbows on his knees, the stick dangling from his hands. In the flickering light, with the bill of his cap pulled low and the fire's glow accentuating the lines on his lean cheeks, he looked seasoned, chiseled to a clear-cut form. I felt he was the kind of man I had come here to know, and I was ready to shake hands on a partnership with him.

I asked him about the country over there, what it was like. He came out of himself and replied in the same quiet, absorbed voice as before.

"They say it's really beautiful. Not so much right around salt water. That's mostly flat, endless stretches of flatland, tundra, and pothole lakes. But two guys who fished over there a few years ago told me north of Dillingham it's all forests and mountains, and there's a long chain of clear-water lakes that's still pure wilderness. It's real big country, spectacular as anything left anywhere in the world. There's only a couple of native fish camps in there and maybe some Eskimos hunting or trapping up from Dillingham or the villages along the Nushagak River. It's wide open and wild."

Les knew what I was after, why I had come to Alaska that summer of 1963. He eyed me and passed the bottle.

"How about game?" I asked. "Is it good game country? You know, that's important—" I hesitated, not wanting to come across as though I was trying to sound like an old-timer "—I mean, can a man figure on feeding his family?"

The fire reflected in his glasses, and where his eyes had been, flames danced as he spoke.

"Moose and black bear all over the place—and some grizzly too: though you might be less interested in eating him than making sure he doesn't eat you." He laughed again, with a whoop, white teeth flashing. "And in the northern parts there's caribou. And if you like fish, well, those lakes and streams are so thick with hungry char, rainbow, and grayling you have to hide behind a tree to bait your hook. Then there's the salmon every year, too. And there's fur . . ."

He paused and reached for the bottle—the jug.

"Wolves?" I asked, as he probably expected I would. To me, as to many people, the wolf was type and symbol of the old wild life. The chance to live near such animals, just to know they were there, wild and freely roaming the land, even if I never saw or heard them, seemed a rare privilege in a world where everything wild and free was being destroyed or turned into dollars. I knew I would never kill a wolf. I knew I needed them.

"Wolves? Hell, yes." Les smiled. He had wanted to know the same sort of things ten years earlier. "There's wolves in most every part of Alaska as wild as Bristol Bay. And there'll be wolverine, fox, mink, otter, marten, probably lynx, too, where there's rabbits."

My mind was spinning out, from his words more than from the booze. He painted a picture of what I wanted: a country where wild animals outnumbered tame people. I had rejected the famed Kenai Peninsula outright, with its real estate agents and No Trespassing signs, roads and power lines, and therefore amenities—creature comforts, as they say—and therefore fender fishermen and four-by-four hunters and people outnumbering everything but the mosquitoes. I would settle for nothing less than wilderness. If I was going to go at all, I needed to go all the way. Living *near* wilderness wasn't good enough: I needed to live *in* wilderness. In cities, suburbs, and the domesticated countryside you are in the mind of modern man, an unhealthy environment. In wilderness you are in the aboriginal mind, which can teach you something else.

That was what I was after. Not Father Abraham's but Mother Nature's bosom, not money and things but life "as cold and passionate as the dawn" (W. B. Yeats).

❁

The following spring, before the end of May, having graded all final exams, term papers, and dissertations in record time, I was back in Alaska. Les and I had corresponded over the winter, and he was there to meet me at the rudimentary Kenai airport. He grinned when he saw me, the first passenger out of the plane. We drove to his little frame house on a lake off the graveled North Road, out of the town of Kenai.

Our plan was to equip his eighteen-foot open skiff with a pair of new outboards and trust that rig to get us to Bristol Bay and the fishing. We would cross Cook Inlet and run down to Iliamna Bay, where Carl Williams would meet us with his big flatbed truck and carry the skiff and us over the mountains to Iliamna Lake; then down the one hundred miles or so of the lake, Alaska's largest, to the Kvichak River, which, seventy miles downstream, empties into the Naknek/Kvichak watershed of Bristol Bay; from thence the ten-hour run around the horn into Nushagak Bay and up to the port of Dillingham at the head of the bay. Les traced the route with a callused finger on a large map spread out under a kerosene lamp on the floor of his house. It seemed to me a tremendous journey—in an open skiff, a hazardous adventure, a test of nerve and stamina. I had seen Cook Inlet, and I could imagine the rest. But I was ready to go, prepared to risk everything, life included, to get there, to prove up as an Alaskan and a fisherman, to take the first step toward realizing my vision of a new life in the north woods.

But fate had other plans for us than the open skiff.

❀

Perched on a trailer by the side of a back road we happened to be on one day was a boat for sale—a small boat, but much larger than Les's skiff. And it had a cabin. I saw the For Sale sign, weathered red paint on a slab of board, tacked onto the stern.

"Whoa!" I cried out as we passed. "There's a *boat* for sale—and it's got a cabin!"

Les glanced in the rearview mirror, put his foot on the brake, and turned the car around. We got out to look her over. The year before, while making plans around the campfire, Les had mentioned the possibility of picking up a good used fish boat, if we could find one cheap enough for our budget; if not, we would go for it in the skiff he used for his setnetting operation in Chinitna Bay. Then the great earthquake of 1964 intervened, which sank or wrecked so many boats that it wiped out the market for an affordable buy in a used fish boat.

This one was not a fish boat. It was homemade out of fiberglassed plywood, with the severed top of an automobile—car windows and all—for a cabin roof. The hull was dark green, the superstructure light gray. It had been built, we later learned, to cruise one of Alaska's larger lakes, and for that use it was well designed: twenty-seven feet long, narrow of beam, powered by a dependable Willys marine conversion. It could sleep two, three in a pinch. The cabin was plain but comfortable, with a two-burner stove, a sink—and even a toilet, or head, tucked under a seat.

Part of my subsequent initiation into the real thing in Bristol Bay was learning to regard—and use—a bucket as a toilet. No frilly cabins on the old commercial hulls, no catering to creature comforts on those tough ships. Fishing wasn't supposed to be easy or fun: Fishing was business. Crew's quarters were typically two narrow bunks, an oil cookstove, maybe a sink, and at least half the exposed engine jutting into the cabin, smelling of gas and oil and sounding like the Industrial Revolution, all of it crammed into the narrow forward third of the hull. As the name implies, a fish boat was designed for fish, not for fishermen. Before this type of boat, which was common in Bristol Bay during the sixties, back in the really old days the double-ended sailboats used were totally bereft of *any* kind of cabin, much less a flush toilet. In fact the hardy sailboat fisherman reputedly scorned even so modest a compromise with convenience as the bucket, choosing instead to squat over the side. This might have provided the compensatory amenity of a bidet effect in those rough and splashy waters (it's an ill wind that blows no good), although even in this regard a certain hardihood was needed, inasmuch as the waters of Bristol Bay never warm to the ardent but brief kiss of the summer sun.

Those sailboat fishermen weren't the last to go down to the sea in little more than boots and slicker. All through the sixties, among the many new fiberglass fish boats with cabins like motel rooms, there were scattered the redoubtable mosquito fleet: the skiff fishermen. Powered by fast outboards, many a skiff made it into port at the end of the day, like coming home from work. But even those commuters occasionally, and many a skiff fisherman habitually, would be adrift on big water in all kinds of weather, sometimes for days, during a long open period or maybe needing the money and scratching hard for a few fish before or after the run. At best they might have a "doghouse" to crawl into—a section of the bow decked over, with maybe an old cotton mattress, more than likely damp, and a decrepit sleeping bag. They would fish until exhausted, gulp down a can of cold beans or whatever, and crawl into the doghouse to lapse into oblivion, still wearing boots and slicker.

I was eager to avoid that sort of thing if possible. The journey to Dillingham would likely take a week or two; Iliamna Lake and Bristol Bay generally had had reputations for stormy weather; we would have to sleep on board whatever craft carried us to Dillingham; and I might never have another go at it if we didn't make it that year. I saw in this little cabin cruiser with the For Sale sign a chance to better the odds. It could be my ticket to ride, could get us to Bristol Bay and the fishing. From there it would be a much shorter step into the wilderness.

It was a clear day, still and warm. The boat seemed, in my eyes, to be basking in the sunshine like a starlet under floodlights, glowing and preternaturally attractive. The gravel road was rarely traveled; why the boat had been parked in that spot we had no idea. To me it *did* seem almost providential. I was ready to believe it was there because I needed it, just as Les had appeared when I needed him: Ask, and it shall be given unto thee.

VanDevere walked around her, checking her out, stooping and peering. Being familiar with the makings of a real fish boat, he was dubious about this lady. But the hull seemed sound, no breaks in the fiberglass, only a few nicks in the propeller. He judged it hadn't been used much and was probably no more than a few years old. The engine under the hatch was frozen up from lack of use and proper care, but that could be fixed, and it too looked in fair shape generally. He was interested, despite the oddball, almost ridiculous cabin top. The For Sale sign bore a name and Anchorage telephone number. The phone lines to Anchorage were still out of service from the quake, but the road around Turnagain Arm had just been reopened. We would make the drive up to the big city in Les's Volkswagen and see what came of it.

❀

Life loses a measure of normalcy when you are suffering the booze-inspired racies in the kitchen of a small Alaskan house about four-thousand miles away from home, on the verge, moreover, of taking a giant and possibly irreversible step into the great unknown. We had stayed up late with our host, the boat's owner, swapping lies, as they say in Alaska, bargaining, and drinking, but we hadn't been able to strike a deal. Everything was still up in the air when we crashed.

In the silence of the sleeping house, my revved-up heart sounded so loud I was afraid its thumping, combined with the ungovernable squishes and rumblings coming from my stomach, might actually awaken Les, who was sleeping, I hoped, only a few feet away. Now, were he to wake up and find me, like Shane, standing hatless in the rain outside with my arms folded across my buckskin chest, lost in somber thoughts, it would have been all right. But to be found thumping and gurgling half under a Sears Roebuck table was not according to Alaskan macho.

My mind, however, could not be slowed down. It ran all the red lights, ignored the stop signs, rammed the barricades. For all I knew or was ready to believe, the northern lights, a phenomenon inexplicable even to science then, were running amok like crazed photons down avenues moonbeams had not yet traveled into my susceptible brain cells. Maybe these mysterious lights of the northland were psychic invaders generating bad nerves, Sasquatch stories, and a taste for booze—or maybe generating not only Sasquatch stories but Sasquatches: palpable manifestations of the repressed fear of wild nature. Hadn't there been a movie based on a similar idea, about psychic energies becoming physical forces and tearing people apart?

Half of all Alaskans in those days had proved themselves vulnerable to moonbeams by virtue of their infatuation with life on the Last Frontier. Outrageous romantics, their heads were filled with images from John Wayne movies and Robert Service verses. For them, Alaska was the land of adventure: "Nowth to Alaskah!" The other half were the realists, the money people. Their minds were Brinks vans impervious to moonbeams. The moon itself, to them, was neither Diana the Huntress nor the goddess Astarte, nor even the blue moon of lovers or the full moon of werewolves. It was nothing but a worthless slag heap in an empty sky. Their heads were filled with images from *Fortune* magazine. For them Alaska was the land of opportunity: Get in first and get all you can!

I belonged unequivocally with the outrageous romantics. The idea of making money out of the Great Land never occurred to me. I dreamed of wilderness; of log cabins glowing in the sun on the shores of sky blue waters; of wolves howling at the winter moon; of a silence so deep you could hear the Great Spirit breathing; of clean rivers, clear lakes, and streams full of fish; of mountains, valleys, and tundra untouched by the tools of civilization, unspoiled by the filth of the insane factory—of a wild, free, natural world.

So I lay awake in the middle of the night in a sleeping bag on the floor of the boatbuilder's house in Anchorage, worried that our offer for his creation would be rejected. The owner's pride, because he was also the romantic builder of boat dreams, had been offended by our necessarily minimal offer for his craft (it was all the money I had). But by morning his realistic better half, a hard-eyed, taciturn woman who appeared to be altogether free of any kind of romance, had triumphed, no doubt persuading him by force of the popular mandate favoring the dollar in the hand over the maybes in the bush. I had cash; the deal went through like osmosis.

*Port N Storm* we called the boat: any port in a storm. Because if it wasn't the boat we wanted, it was the boat we got. Les remained doubtful about it but was willing to gamble, and he agreed that life would surely be warmer and drier on my *Port N*

*Storm* than in his open skiff. He regarded her (boats are always female to men, because they love them) from the point of view of hard reality and found her wanting: not broad enough in the beam, too small-boned for the life we planned for her. She was a funky suburbanite, and we needed a sturdy country lass. But I saw her from the superior position of romance, and from that vantage point she looked down-home and comely. I liked her right away. I liked her plain but graceful lines and the touch of comfort in her hold. I could see Les and me in the snug cabin sipping coffee while the wind outside blew cold and rocked us on the water. Nothing did I care, in my sky blue mind, that some macho wave might overwhelm her, pick her up and drop her onto a bar, breaking a good deal more than her heart, nor that the iron embrace of a scow in sloppy weather might crack her spare ribs. Les was thinking along those lines as he stood back with lidded eyes, but he was the silent type. My romance with the lady burned undiminished until we burst onto the serious seas of Bristol Bay, and vice versa.

We towed *Port N Storm* to the lake just off a spur of the North Road out of Kenai, where Les had built his house. The boat, looking big and sleek with all her hull exposed, something like a submarine, rested on the trailer off to the side of the road a stone's throw from the water. It struck me that this boat was more than an amorphous wish or dream: She was real, solid— yet somehow aloof, looking away, not saying. She would promise nothing. But she had been in water; you could see the gray line of it on her hull. And she would be in water again soon, I hoped, only this time it would be salt water, big water, not just some inland lake with a fringe of summer places.

Before we could go a-sailing into the storied waters of Bristol Bay, however, we had to get the Willys engine running properly. It had unfrozen readily enough and would run, but there was a flat spot in the low range of acceleration. The trip ahead of us was too imposing to be undertaken with a faulty engine; if we couldn't get it running right, we wouldn't be going—all the money we had was in the boat, with none left for new outboards for the skiff. Les tried everything he knew about engines, but for a week he couldn't understand what was causing the problem in the acceleration. I was no help to him, other than to haul buckets of water from the lake to the tubs that substituted for the lake in Les's rigged cooling system. I knew nothing about engines. (Once, when a mechanic informed me I had blown a head gasket, it sounded so bad I asked what he thought the car would bring as junk.)

As a last resort, we drove into Kenai to consult an old mechanic Les knew. They sat opposite each other, going over the problem like a couple of physicians discussing a difficult case, the older, Lionel Barrymore figure asking the questions, listening, pondering. I couldn't follow them, much less offer suggestions; they had their own language. I could only hang there on the tenterhooks of my ignorance. Then finally the old guy made his diagnosis, and Les brightened. He slapped his knee. "Damn! I never thought of that."

They had figured it out. We would be going! I felt like a death-row case granted a last-minute reprieve. We left in high spirits.

❁

Kenai at that time was small, flat, half done. Everything was geared to survival: little (easy-to-heat) two-by-four buildings hugging the ground; hardware and lumber stores, bulldozers and backhoes everywhere; gravel or dirt roads without sidewalks; houses and mobile homes that were merely shelters, without lawns or gardens. Civic beauty was not even a topic of conversation. Women gave one another tool chests for Christmas. The thing was to get and maintain the machines that would conquer the wilderness, or at least hold it at bay. Technology was the ultimate weapon, and Kenai was where you went to get it. The modern American dream of freedom on the frontier rode on ball bearings.

Respite from the battle and a bit of sentiment could also be had in Kenai, at the bars, where the men with spruce pitch on their pants and grease lines in their hands came in the evening to soak up the booze, the soft colored lights, and the music about false loves and broken hearts. They would have liked a little sex, too—it hung in the air of those places like a forlorn hope—but sex in a land of many men and few women was harder to get than drunk. So they got drunk, and talked about machines and women, becoming really sincere with one another as the night progressed and the late-middle-aged ex-dancer who ran the place got predictably younger.

During the next several days, now that the engine was fixed, we lowered the plywood deck aft of the engine hatch so it could hold the nets and fish, and constructed "picking bins," three-quarter-inch exterior plywood partitions forward of the stern hold, one on each side, with a third bin in between into which the net was pulled as the fish got picked out of the webbing.

Actually, as I was soon to learn, the term "picking fish" is a misnomer. Extracting salmon from the tangled multi-ply nylon mesh, which catches them by the gills, nose, teeth, fins, back, belly, or tail, or all of the above, is not at all like picking flowers or berries. It is hard and often frustrating work. Each of the fish will weigh from a few pounds to the occasional king (chinook) at thirty or forty pounds, and there may be a dozen of them entangled in the fathom of net hanging between you and your partner standing in the bin opposite, some of them still struggling and tied in Gordian knots. With three nets ("shackles," as they're called) laid out, on a good day there may be one or two thousand fish to "pick."

Finally Les investigated the Kenai dump and, having an inventive mind, retrieved most of the flotsam and jetsam necessary to fabricate a stern roller—hand powered—over which the nets roll out and get pulled back into the boat. We painted it the same color gray as the boat's superstructure. It looked pretty good to me, professional. I had never seen a Bristol Bay gillnetter with its steel-and-rubber hydraulic power roller with hoses and piping. To me the homemade wooden roller was the final touch. *Port N Storm* was no longer a mere pleasure craft. She was a fish boat.

❖

Nights after working on the boat until we were just too tired (it stayed light until around midnight), I stretched out on an army cot upstairs—or more exactly up-ladder—in the tiny unfinished attic of the frame house Les had built. It was very quiet. There were no nearby neighbors. I could hear even the slight flutter of the candle. The loons out on the lake called at intervals, their cries seeming uncanny to me, and a little unnerving. They came across as the alien, inhuman voice of this strange land: Whatever else they signified, I knew in those cries that this land was not human-hearted, was not safe, was not sweet, was not Disney. This land and its strong spirit were a reality to be reckoned with. It was then that doubts sometimes paced the perimeters of my mind and fear stood in the shadows. Did I really know what I was doing, to be running counter to the charted direction of our whole civilization? To be putting my family at risk? Was my obsession with a new life in the woods sensible, or even feasible? Feasible for *me*, I meant: I knew other men had done it, but I didn't know if I could. I hadn't the background; I lacked training or experience in the skills required. Les had built this house; all I had ever built was a doghouse, and it wasn't well built. Was I not simply another starry-eyed romantic, an armchair adventurer, on the verge of throwing away everything the world holds dear—tenured professorship; the lovely, comfortable farm; the social prestige and security; maybe even lose one of my family to unexpected perils—in

search of what? A daydream movie projected out of vague longings and the words of mystics and poets—poets who, according
to Plato, are liars. Certainly most of my friends and family
thought I was crazy, not just in terms of "oh you crazy guy" but
clinically insane: to *want* to go *back* to outhouses, kerosene
lamps, and bare subsistence! Not to mention bears, wolves, mosquitoes, and subzero temperatures. In the race for riches that was
the normal world, I was driving in reverse without benefit of a
rearview mirror. Some nights when the loons called, it seemed
very likely that my friends and family were right. I heard my
mother's voice: "How can you *think* of taking those lovely children and depriving them of a future, to live in . . . *wilderness!*"
To them wilderness meant something utterly different from what
it meant to me. Wilderness to them was something like chaos,
something unformed, undeveloped, a deprivation, where life was
surely nasty, brutish, and short. They were among the American
faithful who believed that money and happiness were synony-
mous, and they couldn't see us getting much of either in the
wilderness. But I believed that happiness was life lived as poetry,
as nearly as possible in the old, spiritual consciousness, in intimate bodily connection with an earth that was a living, sacred
being; and I hoped and trusted that living in the woods would
revive that old consciousness, now dormant, repressed. Subsistence, the elemental life, didn't mean privation to me: quite the
contrary. In a world where "More!" is the cry on everyone's lips,
no matter how very much they already have, mere subsistence
held for me the promise of fulfillment. "More!" wrote Blake, "is
the cry of a mistaken soul."

Now I had placed my bet, laid my money down. The die was
about to be cast, and I felt that it was very likely to be for mortal
stakes. I had done well enough in the civilized world, according
to its own criteria, but I had found it wanting. Could I do as
well in the primeval world, or would it find *me* wanting? Was
there still enough of a real human being left in me to *see* that
world? Was I on the verge of burning bridges when I hadn't yet
set foot on the other side?

Thoughts like these were not conducive to sleep. But neither were the other kind, the ebullient ones: that I was going for it, heading out, sailing down to Bristol Bay, the first leg of the journey to that other world, that other me.

The siren song that lured me didn't broadcast on the frequencies of bank accounts and retirement plans. It said nothing of security of any kind but whispered promises of splendor, rumors of glory—"the hour of splendor in the grass and glory in the flower."

❁

After about two weeks of work on the boat we were ready to go. We drove into town to buy grub for the trip, feeling high, needing all the gravity we could get to maintain contact with the ground. The day, sunny and bright with a sharp wind tossing the spruce and birch by the road, mirrored our mood. Beyond the trees the blue waters of Cook Inlet were frothed with great expectations.

With Les's monetary contribution to the expedition, we filled shopping carts with canned goods, coffee, pancake mix, a slab of bacon; kidding around, poking each other in the ribs, standing head and shoulders above the other shoppers, who weren't going. Then we bought a case of booze and drove back well above the speed limit (and the road) and pulled up to *Port N Storm* trailing clouds of dust and glory. We stowed our gear on board, the grub and booze, shaving gear, toilet paper, wool shirts and sweaters, jeans, hip boots and rain gear, long johns, several pairs of socks, my Winchester 30.06 and Ruger Blackhawk .44 magnum, Les's 12-gauge shotgun, and my Martin guitar. (Why all the firepower? In those days Alaska was Wild West country.) It all tucked away very nicely in the various bins and the one narrow closet. With the water tank filled, the bottle of propane hooked up, and Les's old tube-type marine radio installed and connected to the antenna, *Port N Storm* was shipshape and ready to sail. As we walked toward the house, I turned to see her silhouetted against the long light of the evening sky, her sharp bow cutting into the ribbed and luminous clouds as though she were cruising the sky, voyaging into a world of light.

That night, lying on the army cot listening to the loons, I stared up into the darkness, and sleep became a fugitive I couldn't find until, near dawn, too tired to care, sleep found me.

❁

The next morning broke fair, the smell of the damp woods and the lake cool and strong on the air. After breakfast Les, feeling awkward, uncertain, laughed a lot saying good-bye to his wife and son while I carried out the last of our stuff. We had split a huge pile of seasoned birch and dead spruce for them. Betty cried a little and said we should be real careful over there and come back safe. "Hey," Les said, and glanced down at his son, who looked as if he would cry too if he thought it would be okay, "next year maybe we'll all get to go over there together. But Bob and I need to see what it's like first, right?" The boy looked up and managed a small smile and a nod.

And then we were out the door and into the car, glad to be on our way, just the two men, like two boys again, free for a while from family ties and cares, free to go exploring into terra incognita.

We towed *Port N Storm* along the empty road to the Nikiski dock, where Les worked occasionally and knew the foreman. For the price of a complimentary jug the foreman activated his launching boom, lifted *Port N Storm* off the trailer, with Les and me standing on deck in midair, and lowered her into salt water. We were afloat. She rode the swells like a regular boat. A group of workers up on the dock looked down and waved. Sensing that this was a maiden voyage, they wished us well.

Les started the engine and we turned slowly away from the

dock, heading into a movie with a cast of thousands and sets costing millions of years.

We rounded the point of land protecting the dock area, with me now at the wheel, and smacked right into the actual sea. *Port N Storm* met the first real wave of her life with all the innocence of a virgin emissary to Genghis Khan—and with similar consequences. The wave hit her like a broadax and she crashed into the trough. The shock of it ran through her body and up my legs and rattled my bones like dice. Then the next wave hit dead on, and the world washed out in spray. I hung on to the wheel. Les had gone below for something, but he was up on deck before wave three. He cut the throttle way down.

"Jesus Christ," he said.

It hadn't occurred to me to slow down. I had a lot to learn, and this was obviously a school of hard knocks. But I was signed up and had paid my tuition and was ready to take the course.

❖

When I had studied maps of Alaska back at my farm, I figured the west side of Cook Inlet, which was roadless and largely uninhabited, would be worth exploring. Toward that end, in 1963 on my first pilgrimage to Alaska, I towed along my fourteen-foot aluminum Starcraft—a rowboat, in fact, with a little five-horse outboard on the stern. That rig wouldn't even have been capable of holding steady against the tide, no less of crossing the inlet. Big ships founder and swamp in Cook Inlet. Nobody who deals with it is casual about it. The skiff-and-kicker rigs used by some fishermen, like Les, are well designed from long experience to handle big water. They are apt to be twenty or more feet long, wide-beamed, and pushed by powerful, fast engines with able men at the controls who are careful to get weather reports and very deliberate as to when they set forth. (Unless, of course, they have been drinking.)

I was glad we had *Port N Storm*, but even so the journey

wasn't likely to be a simple pleasure cruise. After all, we would be on our own in a huge uncivilized arena where the combative elements had not been bred on the milk of human kindness.

Les figured it was too rough to start across that evening, so after running south for an hour or so we anchored in a protective cove. We were both so high at being on our way at last, on board and away from it all in the simple world of boats and weather, with who-knew-what adventures awaiting us, that we killed a fifth of Jim Beam between us and gobbled up two whole cans of Planters salted peanuts mainly just sitting opposite one another, feeling the motion of the boat, smelling the sea, talking Bristol Bay and eventually, of course, women.

Later, in the darkness, as we rode the easy swells into the night, I lingered on the edge of consciousness, more or less drunk, and images out of Walt Whitman rose and fell in my mind. Men in wool sweaters and watch caps, ruddy from the weather, tough but good-natured, fishermen, bushmen, too care-less to be mean but too much themselves to be pushed around, men who did their own thinking, at home in their lives, rooted in nature, sleeping with both legs well stretched out; and women too, sturdy, strong-minded, in every way the men's equal, adrift on the currents of their femininity, in touch with the earth, confident in the daily tasks of their lives. Ah, was there in fact such a brave new world that had such people in it, here in the northland, down in Bristol Bay? I believed there was.

❀

The next day dawned fair again, but just a bit calmer. We were both hungover, yet eager to get going. After coffee, but without the bacon and pancakes, we weighed anchor (it was heavy) and eased out into the inlet. The breeze was fresh, welcome and clarifying with the tang of salt, but the white-capping waves sent shock troops up the avenues of our spines and into the sensitive suburbs of our skulls. Two-thirds of *Port N Storm*'s bottom was flatter than we could appreciate, and despite her lithe appearance she was heavy-footed in a chop. We proceeded slowly, with all due respect for her shortcomings and our wounded sensibilities.

Everything around us, however, was sparkling and not to be denied. Amid the blue of it, white balls of cloud bounced cleaner than a Winslow Homer watercolor. Black mergansers and white gulls whirled and dipped in a calligraphic yin and yang. Off the starboard bow the white backs of a school of beluga whales, fairly abundant in Cook Inlet, appeared and disappeared among the waves.

VanDevere took a sly proprietary pride in this scene. He lounged at the wheel and glanced over at me now and again, vicariously seeing it all through my new eyes. Actually, Captain Cook himself could not have regarded it with greater admiration than we did, nor could his view have taken in much that was different from our own. The west side of Cook Inlet in 1964 was the same as it had always been, even before the first Eskimo hunted along its shores. A pterodactyl landing on one of the ridges above us wouldn't have seemed out of place. The ragged rocks, the booming surf, the strip of beach, and the forest primeval. It was large scale, imposing—man hadn't even begun to subdue it—and it was, in a subtle way, unnerving. Especially when after the impact of a particularly hard-hitting wave the engine suddenly quit. I looked quickly at Les, ship's engineer.

"Fuck!" he said.

The wind was drifting us in for a close-up of the rocks. Les threw open the hatch cover and started fiddling with the engine. I stood by the wheel, reluctant to distract him with questions, although I had some, because what he was doing seemed very important. But I was on the verge of mentioning, calmly of course, that we were rapidly approaching the rocks, when he straightened up and hit the starter button. The engine cranked for a second or two, then purred into life. I swung the wheel, and *Port N Storm* turned away from the shore. The artificial sound of the engine at that moment was far more gratifying and pleasing to my ears than the natural sound of the surf crashing against the rocks. Les muttered something about cleaning the goddamn settling bowl, which I didn't understand at the time.

❀

After about two days of mostly fair weather we were abreast of Chinitna Bay, where Les setnet each summer. As we pushed slowly past the mouth of the bay, he stood watching, and when we could no longer see his little plywood fish camp on the north shore, he told me he had never been south of Chinitna Bay before, that from that point on the water would be unfamiliar to us both.

"So you might as well take the wheel," he said, "while I go below and see if I can figure out from the chart how we're going to know when we get to Iliamna Bay."

I must have looked a little startled: *I* take the wheel now, and he goes below?

He grinned. "Just stay about this far offshore—and don't drive too fast."

Well, if it was all right with him, it was all right with me too. Mine wasn't the only life on board we could lose.

Les studied the chart, but as he suspected, the entrance to Iliamna Bay was half concealed and tricky to identify. It didn't directly front the inlet but sneaked in almost parallel, behind a bluff. From a little distance you couldn't readily tell there was a bay in there at all. The shoreline appeared unbroken. But Les had it figured, and we eased in close enough to make out the entrance. To get to the rear of the bay, back and around a rocky headland, we had to wait for the floodtide. The earthquake had jostled things around so much, Les wasn't willing to trust the chart as to the locations of big rocks. Once in there, we would have to let the tide go out from under us, the boat settling into what we hoped would be mud.

It was at the far end of the bay that the only road in the entire region came down out of the mountains to the water. The state had engineered the gravel road as a connection between Cook Inlet and Iliamna Lake. Its purpose, as far as I ever understood, was to provide precisely the usage to which we hoped to put it—to transport fishermen and their boats from Cook Inlet to Bristol Bay, and vice versa. Without this passage, getting a boat to Bristol Bay from Cook Inlet would have required a horrendous journey down half the length of the Alaska Peninsula and back up the other side. The storms in those exposed waters are prodigious, and because the trip would take weeks, the chances of encountering one were very good.

But neither was this shortcut over the mountains entirely a matter of course. The road climbs steeply from the bay, twisting and turning, and keeps on climbing high into the Chigmit Mountains. From the summit the river down in the valley looks like a piece of tinsel. The high pass had been cleared of snow, we were to learn, but conditions were still marginal.

A man named Carl Williams was in charge of the road at that time. We had arranged by mail for him to meet us with his big flatbed truck on or about June 3. Schedules in that country were necessarily flexible; everything depended on the weather and the resulting conditions.

The head of the bay contained nothing human-made other than the end of the road and a small wooden dock with a boom-and-tackle rig. We had slipped in carefully with the flood and anchored about twenty yards offshore. As *Port N Storm* slowly dropped with the ebbing tide, Les and I probed with the oar and boat hook around and beneath the boat for rocks, but found none. We settled down nice and level in the mud. All we had to do now was wait.

It was still afternoon when the tide went out—literally, right out of this far end of the bay, around the corner of the bluff, and out of sight. There was nothing left but sandy gray mud. The bottom, however, looked firm enough for walking. We

didn't want to just sit around on board waiting, so we pulled on
our boots and decided to go exploring. The area was known for
its grizzly population, and the shore was dense with willows. So
we each took along a big gun. I also strapped on my .22 handgun.

We were looking over the dock area when we heard soft
cluckings coming from the willows. "That sounds like the dinner
bell," Les said with a straight face. He started for the willows.
He was carrying a 12-gauge pump shotgun, considered a good
bear gun at close range but also okay for birds a ways off. I toted
my Winchester 30.06 with a tip-off mount. (In dense cover and
at short distances, a scope is worse than useless because all you
would see through it would be magnified branches and leaves
and a patch of hair from no telling what part of the animal's
body.)

The possibility of a close encounter of any kind with a bear
didn't worry me then. That's what I had come for, something
like that: not to prove myself, even to myself, although that was
probably part of it, seeking a rite of passage, but mainly as I saw
it danger, simple immediate physical danger, had always been a
part of the real life of our species. Being terrified and maybe
mauled and killed by a bear was an element in the composition
of the good life our ancestors had led for a million years. Danger
had pedigree, authenticity. I much preferred it to the gnawing
anxieties of our time. And why shouldn't humans, who kill and
eat so many animals, be killed and eaten too? Turnabout is fair
play. (How *careful* we are about our own lives, the lives of *people*,
and how cavalier about the lives of the other animals.)

I had read enough to understand that the grizzly bear was a
most formidable animal. Even the scientific nomenclature gave
you fair warning: *Ursus horribilis,* the horrible bear. By all accounts, a grizzly is a portion of nature that has remained intrac-
tably indifferent or hostile to the will of man, going its own way,
inviolably itself, even unto extinction. Touch the wrong button
and the bear goes off. Its temper is instantaneous and unmod-

ulated. It doesn't stop to think things over and wouldn't count to ten if it knew how.

One of the wrong buttons on the bear's panel of responses is surprise. It doesn't like to be surprised by other fairly large animals, such as man. It may bolt or it may charge. In the latter case, if the charge is real and not just a warning bluff, there may be little time to calculate a proper reaction. Big as they are, bears are quick as cats when they decide to go for you. As we walked into the willows toward the clucking sounds, Les jacked a shell into the chamber of his shotgun, and I did likewise with my 30.06.

Under the canopy of willow tops over our heads, the earth was a fine gray sand, dry and soft as dust. The delicate shadows of the leaves patterned the ground like camouflage. The cluckings had stopped. Then about a dozen ptarmigan were suddenly there, just a few feet ahead of us. They wore their beautiful white-and-auburn summer plumage, which blended in marvelously with the dappled ground. They must have been feeding and dusting themselves. Being unfamiliar with man, they didn't scurry off or rocket away as their cousin the partridge would do, but merely stood inquisitively, cocking their heads, or strutted about nervously a few paces. Even after I had started shooting with the handgun and one of them flopped about while dying, they seemed unsure of what was happening. I got three of them before the rest decided the area was unhealthy and took off. Then Les fired, and another bird fell.

We collected the downed birds and followed after the flock, pushing through the willows. After maybe a hundred yards, simultaneously we abruptly stopped. Ahead of us was a large tangled mound of brush against the side of a hill. The air was rank with an odor like the armpits of a scared man. For an instant I thought the odor might be my own, because when my eyes fell on that mound and my nostrils caught the smell, a voice in my head said *bear* and my stomach did an adrenaline flip. The breeze was in our faces, and it rustled the leaves overhead loudly enough to cover the sound of our movements. Les shook his head and started backing away, his gun at the ready. We weren't after bear and hoped the feeling was mutual. That smell gave promise of extremely uncivilized behavior, and it excited in me a flush of feelings no doubt equally primitive.

That what we had smelled very likely had been a bear, or at least a bear den, seemed confirmed the next morning. The tide was out, and the glistening mud between *Port N Storm* and shore was stitched with the pigeon-toed tracks of a big grizzly. It had crossed recently, while we slept. The breeze was onshore, and the tracks showed where it had milled about, catching a sniff of us, perhaps, and then moved off into the willows. We were glad the bear's curiosity or nose hadn't brought it close enough to smell our slab of bacon. It might have climbed on board to have some. Bears frequently investigate (that is, search and destroy) parked boats and airplanes. If Carl Williams didn't show that day, we figured we had best sleep one at a time that night.

Meanwhile, inasmuch as it was a warm and sunny afternoon and we had nothing to do but wait, having feasted on the birds, we decided to stretch out on deck, maybe siesta a little, Les in the stern and I alongside the engine hatch. The deck was warm and the sun hot in the stillness. There was no sound at all, not even a mosquito. The sky, a perfectly blank blue, had nothing to say. The sun's heat penetrated the wool of my shirt, pressed through the thin denim on my legs, and sank to the marrow, loosening the strings holding body and mind together. I began to drift off. Scattered lines from a poem came to me: "Here where the world is quiet; / Here where all trouble seems / Dead winds' and spent waves' riot in doubtful dream of dreams . . ." Something like that. Tennyson? Browning? Swinburne? One of those Victorians, drowsing after dinner by the fire.

I heard something close by, right next to the boat, a sound like lips smacking softly, and I thought I felt the boat move. I spiraled up into alertness. What was that so close, touching the boat? Then at once I knew it was water, softly lapping. This twenty-foot tide, this gigantic power, had rounded the corner of the bluff like a cat and now touched *Port N Storm* as with a tentative paw.

I had never before quite heard—had never perhaps been in quite the right emptiness of mind to hear—that particular sound of water. The delicacy of it, because I was aware of its power, seemed almost insidious. The boat moved ever so slightly. The lapping continued, as delicate as before, but a little stronger, less hesitant. Then with a series of small nudges *Port N Storm* was lifted and afloat. When I got up and looked over the side, the bay was filled with water. And in the distance, from up in the mountains, I heard the sound of motors.

Within the hour Carl Williams appeared, down-gearing for the last sharp descent to the beach. A Jeep came first, driven by a helper, a man so nondescript he almost disappeared before my eyes. Williams was a large, direct man somewhere in his middle years. He wore gray striped coveralls, a peaked cap, and hard-toed workmen's shoes. His hand as we shook was suitably huge and hard.

"Well, you boys is right on time, I see," he smiled, looking at us only in quick, concentrated glances, as though wishing to leave us our space but sizing us up shrewdly according to his lights. "You'll be the first ones over this year. Jesus! We just did make it through the pass, though." He glanced at us and raised his eyebrows. "Still *snow* up there. We had to clear it out of the way. And the shoulders is wet and soft."

I came from the land of regular schedules for trains, planes, and buses, where it was all a matter of course, with perhaps now and then a little irritation of inconvenience when schedules weren't promptly met. Whatever difficulties might be involved remained offstage. Therefore, in this case, the implications of Williams's remarks were lost on me. We had made arrangements to have *Port N Storm* and ourselves transported to Iliamna Lake, and these were the men and machines contracted to do it. Simple as that. It didn't occur to me that such an undertaking in this country wasn't necessarily an unvarying procedure, that it was more in the nature of an adventure than a routine. So I was protected from concern by my ignorance of frontier circumstances. I was ready for adventure anyway, whatever form it might take, and I rested comfortably in their hands.

At the height of the tide, a big one, we moved *Port N Storm* away from the beach and stood ready. Williams backed the long flatbed into the silty water almost to the cab. We made a circle, ruffling the water, and ran the boat up the flatbed as far as she would go. The helper, in hip boots, quickly tied her down, and without, as they say, any further ado we started up into the mountains, with Les and me perched on the engine hatch.

The road was narrow and the ascent from the bay steep. The truck growled and bounced and clawed its way up. We were soon in high, open country. It was strange sitting on a boat watching rocks and tundra go by, but stranger still for me was to see ptarmigan everywhere, in twos and threes, almost within reach. They stood stock-still on the lichen-covered rocks like stuffed birds or else waddled away uncertainly, but they didn't take flight. Back in upper New York State I would hunt all day for a shot or two at a partridge or pheasant. Abundance of game birds like this overloaded my circuits. I wanted to jump off and bag a few, but Les advised me to stay put. Carl Williams wasn't likely to wait while I went a-shooting, even if we managed to communicate my wish over the noise of the engine and wheels, and it was a long walk to Iliamna Lake. I was tempted to go for it anyway and count on catching up, when bits of the shoulder next to the first pair of outside wheels started crumbling away. We had begun the climb into the high pass, cliff rising to the left of us, canyon falling away to the right. The shoulder extended a couple of feet beyond the wheels. Rivulets of melting snow gullied the road. A chunk of shoulder broke off, and we watched the rocks bouncing down toward the narrow valley below. Les looked at me.

"Maybe we could use the exercise," he said.

We jumped off the stern and for the next mile or so jogged behind, watching pieces of the shoulder flake off. After we got through the pass, we hopped back on. We were still far above timberline, but at least there was land on both sides of the road. Williams never slowed down or looked back.

We crossed creeks and small rivers by simply driving through them. On the other side of one of those crystalline streams, Williams stopped and stuck his head out. "You boys see that grizzly back there south of us? Nice yellow one. Big fella. About half a mile off." He didn't wait for a reply but started up again. A capable man, Carl Williams. He saw the game, but I suspected this awesome land was no more than a background he took for granted. The wicked thought crossed my mind that if I could, I would beam him down onto Manhattan's West Side Highway or a main artery in Los Angeles for fifteen minutes during rush hour and then materialize him again in the cab of his truck in this high, wide, and handsome country, compress the changes of hundreds of years into a quarter of an hour, and see what that did to his head.

After a few more tight turns, we began the descent. Soon we were into the trees, a dense forest, almost a jungle, of black spruce. Their hovering mass on either side of us was like a dark green sea poised to obliterate the intruding road. The northern end of Iliamna Lake was rain country, and the woods were solid with growth.

Other than the road itself, there had been no sign of human beings the whole way except for the remnants of a small landing strip, scratched out of a level open stretch, probably by a big-game guide, just before we started down into the forest. *Port N Storm* had crossed the mountains and was heading for the cold, clear waters of Alaska's largest lake, Iliamna, about a hundred miles long and thirty miles across in the middle. Our little lady had come a long way from her summer resort lake near Glen-allen, and she still had a long and unknown way to go before reaching her destination, the port of Dillingham at the head of Nushagak Bay, down in Bristol Bay.

❖

Situated at the northern tip of Iliamna Lake, Pile Bay had once been a native village but was now merely the terminus of the solitary road. There were only the dock and outbuildings for the various machines and generator and, up a short trail from the water, the house where Carl and his wife lived half the year. Entering that shingled frame house was almost like stepping back into nineteenth-century Kansas—an old-fashioned farmhouse with upstairs bedrooms and attic, flowered wallpaper, cast-iron cookstove, large plain rocking chair in the big kitchen, where Williams sat by the CB radio in his coveralls and stout Mrs. Williams in an apron baked bread. So at the end of the wilderness road was not Booneville but Middlesex, not James Fenimore Cooper's Natty Bumpo but Grant Wood's American Gothic. I was to find Alaska full of that kind of incongruity.

But this was still home to wolves—Carl saw them, one a big white male, fairly regularly—and black bear and moose, wolverines and eagles, and all the smaller fauna of the northland. The lake and its feeder streams and rivers held large rainbow trout, sail-finned Arctic grayling, and orange-spotted Arctic char. In the fall the salmon returned, deep red with green heads and undershot jaws and big crooked teeth, to spawn and die in their natal waters. The lake was also home to one of the world's two populations of freshwater seals and, perhaps, to "the monster of Iliamna Lake," some kind of huge creature the pilots of the area spotted near the surface occasionally but were unable to identify before it sank out of sight. The reports were quite consistent about its actuality. Perhaps a sturgeon? No one knew for sure.

*Port N Storm* was unloaded into the water next to Williams's dock, and Les and I slept on board that night. I listened to the rain on the cabin roof and thought about my family back at the farm in New York. This was genuinely wild country—incredibly, in the late twentieth century, still pristine, still unadulterated by industry or commerce, the thing itself—without as yet any evident meddling by humans. My gamble—though for me at the time, privately, it was a certitude—was that country like this was wholesome, our natural habitat, its mere presence tonic. My boys and girls would grow up right as the rain. The family would stay close, depending on and really knowing one another, working together, playing together, shaping a singular purpose, not scattered in all directions like the typical modern family (this prospect of wilderness living was one Carol especially liked). There were only a handful of people in the whole vast area, mostly Eskimo. We would meet and be neighbors to living Eskimo and in their own country—mainly still leading the old life. After all the years of reading Peter Freuchen, Knud Rasmussen, and the other early arctic explorers, years during which the Eskimo stood in my mind as a primary witness to our species' true nature—by all accounts intelligent, good-natured, generous, resourceful, deeply spiritual, and brave—to know them now at firsthand! I hoped my family and I could fit into their lives. Well, tomorrow, I thought, slipping away into sleep, tomorrow we start down the lake, the middle lap of our journey to the fishing grounds of Bristol Bay.

The next morning the sun smiled, if a little wanly, on the bay. Lacy mists drifted across the dark spruce islands and rolled softly over the black water. Les and I were eager to move out, cruise among those islands that seemed to lie shrouded in mystery, beckoning us into another time. We knew we wouldn't encounter any cottages or water-skiers, any anglers in powerboats, colorful flies decorating their hats. We would see, in 1964, nothing more nor less than what the first people had seen. What a privilege—to experience truly wild nature!

Just before we shoved off, Carl handed us a penciled map he

had drawn on a scrap of paper, roughly indicating the way out through the maze of islands. "And watch out, you know, when you get past the islands. It's big water out there." He looked off as though past the islands to the open lake. "A blow will come up real fast in this country, and fact is the lake can get nasty.

"Well." He grinned and stuck out his hand: "Good luck to you boys."

We shook hands all around and then hopped aboard. Les started her up, I undid the lines, and we eased away from the dock. We waved to Williams and his helper, who stood watching, and then we turned to look ahead.

# 2

## GETTING THERE: PHASE 2

*Port N Storm* seemed glad to be in freshwater again, on a lake, her proper element. She sliced through the black sheen with all the elegance of a queen returning to her provinces. Her progress among the crowd of spruce-covered islands seemed swift, effortless, and celebratory. Even Les was impressed, remarking that she would likely be one of the fastest boats in the fishing fleet at Dillingham. (He had never been to Bristol Bay and couldn't know any better.)

We were aiming for the village of Iliamna, formerly Severenson's Landing, on the north side of the lake about fifty miles west. As far as we knew, there were no settlements in between. It occurred to me that if this magnificent piece of real estate were located in New York State, frontage would have been going for a thousand bucks a centimeter, "unimproved."

*Port N Storm* was regal among the islands, but when we passed beyond them the enormity of the great lake opening before us seemed almost to cow her. Her speed appeared reduced, her size diminished, her command rescinded. The lake looked like an inland sea, stretching away in all directions, and I recalled reading that large bodies of freshwater are more dangerous than the salt sea, the water being lighter, more easily whipped up, more hectic. But the day remained calm, beguiling. We continued west through glassy water and slow-drifting fogbanks. A couple of times we lost our bearings in the fog and cut the engine, drifting to a stop in what seemed a dimensionless gray silence, waiting until we could see shore again.

The terrain varied, sometimes gently rolling rocky tundra, sometimes long stretches of spruce and birch woods, fronted with clean sweeps of gravel beach and backed by low mountains and bluffs.

Several hours later we made out the buildings of Iliamna in the distance. Our approach was necessarily of our own devising. There were no marker buoys or channel indicators to guide us among the rocks and small islands off the beach. The human presence was just those few low buildings crouched along the bluff. We picked a spot leeward of a spit of land a bit east of the village and nosed in, swinging broadside to the protected beach.

We needed gas and some repairs we couldn't make ourselves. The shaft of the clutch handle had broken off, and we hoped to get it welded. Les thought it might be a good idea for one of us to stay with the boat: A lot of muddied water had gone under the bridge since the innocent days of Rasmussen and Vilhjalmur Stefansson, and there were some hard feelings among the natives. So I stayed on board while Les went off to see about gas and repairs.

I wasn't really curious to visit the village. I suppose I anticipated no personal relation to it, or perhaps I wasn't ready to approach it or the people—though in a way I wanted to. Yet I felt alien to the place, a stranger-in-a-strange-land feeling. Something about the sparseness of it, as a human settlement, so meager and huddled amongst all the immense raw land, struck me as desolate. It was evening, clouds scudding overhead, the wind off the lake still gray with winter, a band of light low on the melancholy horizon. I wore long johns, sweater, slicker, and watch cap, but I felt chilled standing there on deck gazing out past a couple of islands to the pale sliver of the open lake. This was cold country. It wasn't human-hearted. I felt that it looked at me, if it looked at me at all, with the impersonal gaze of a wolf. Confronted with it now, by myself, I felt daunted. The countryside in New York was mild, comfortable, warm, domesticated, and friendly, like a well-trained dog. This Iliamna country might appear attractive, picturesque, in a calendar photo, but its actual felt presence was forbidding. It wasn't dog but wolf.

This was no place for a summer resort. There was something in the wind inimical to that kind of frivolity. Something would have to change first. Some kind of dread god, a god of the first ages, fierce and unconstrained, occupied this land, and he was heedless of those crouching buildings and the little people who ventured out of them. This land had yet to learn that earth was supposed to be subservient to man, under his dominion. The pure clarity of the water lapping against the boat was invisible except for the rippling refractions of light. That water would have to be dirtied a little before the hot-dog stands and gay umbrellas could sprout along the beach.

Les soon appeared with the welded clutch shaft and one Bob Evans, who had done the welding and now came to claim his reward. We broke out a fifth and filled up our mugs—without benefit of soda, water, ice, or a simple twist of anything but fate. This was the real Alaska, the frontier. Men drank. They drank to get drunk or to kill the bottle, whichever came first. But why? Why the heavy drinking, so typical of men on a frontier? Were they caught between the presence of the wild land whispering freedom, or something scarier, on the one hand, and the constraints of civilization on the other? With booze the great liberator, loosening the ties that bind, conferring the necessary courage? Or were they generically homeless modern hominids, aliens on Earth, feeling the same lonely desolation in the face of naked nature that I had just been feeling, a coldness that only firewater could warm?

As a name "Bob Evans" might just as well have been "Jack Armstrong." But the man behind that name had originally borne another designation not so compatible with the Anglo-Saxon tongue. This young man was Eskimo in blue jeans. Under the Elvis hairdo were the dark-hued features of his people, the broad face, prominent cheekbones, and strong jaw. He said little but drank lots. And as the whiskey disappeared, so did his smile. His eyes became lidded, furtive, his whole aspect sullen and brooding. Not fully aware of what I saw happening, I nevertheless witnessed the sad transformation of Bob Evans into Disinherited Man, and I had my first tentative sip of the bitter cup of cultural dispossession.

But before this sturdy young man deteriorated so far as the borderline between jovial camaraderie and active hostility (*Why have you come to my land? For the fish—for money?*), pronounced footsteps approached along the beach.

I had drunk right along with Bob and Les, and it seemed that each of those footsteps struck the gravel like a declaration or a threat. We sat there in the cabin listening. The footsteps approached decidedly. Whoever or whatever was coming was not wobbling. Les and I exchanged glances. I stood up and went out on deck to see who or what it was. The beach, after all, wasn't a thoroughfare, and there were no other boats around.

The evening had lengthened into dusk. The wind off the lake blew a little harder and colder. *Port N Storm* lurched stiffly against the gravel. The approaching figure loomed large but indistinct in the half-light, a ragged, dark, rectangular form slowly assuming the shape of a man. He wore no hat, and his black jacket was torn and flapping in the wind. His black boots were folded below the knee, the pants above them baggy and black.

He strode directly up to the boat and without pausing or glancing at me marched up the precarious board serving as our gangplank. He wore a broad tight-lipped grin, as though he were suppressing a laugh, and his eyes gleamed. He had curly black hair. He thrust out his hand.

"I hear you're heading for the Nushagak," he said in a deep, oddly clipped, and almost theatrical voice, "and I thought I might be able to keep you from getting drowned."

He burst into a laugh and stood spread-legged, looking at me, one shoulder raised higher than the other, the forearm dangling loose, the elbow cocked—a stance I had never seen or imagined before. A young man, a white man, husky, square-jawed, handsome. A little Clark Kent, glasses and all, a little Errol Flynn, a touch of Quinn the Eskimo. Nothing about this man resembled anything of my colleagues at Syracuse any more than this country resembled anything in upper New York State. He told me his name was Gene Pope.

We went below and opened another fifth.

❁

"Adventure!"

The word filled *Port N Storm*'s tiny cabin like an explosion. It was Pope's word, and as he said it he clenched both fists across his chest and thrust his head and one shoulder forward, baring his teeth, so that the word wasn't so much spoken or even shouted as it was launched—a barbaric yawp flung into the face of prudence, offending the eardrums of decorum, wounding timidity's sensibility, outraging the ladies sipping cocoa in the parlor.

It came across to me as a kind of challenge, a provocation. I had been feeling downcast from the comfortless scene out there on the lake and had been thinking of home, the lawn in the evening, the fireflies winking in the orchard, ice cubes tinkling in the whiskey sours.

"Adventure!" Pope bellowed, in what connection I couldn't tell. He was looking straight at me, and I knew he meant more by that word than running wild and scenic rivers or conquering statistically high mountains, more than voyaging into space, when the calculations are propitious, more even than exploring inner space, though that meaning came near. It seemed to me he meant a way of living, with gusto and without trying to know beforehand, without worrying about being safe, life as a kind of sustained brinkmanship, where just over the brink was sudden death—adventuring upon life itself. I watched him. Energy radiated from him like heat from a stove. He sat next to Evans, both men broad-shouldered, deep-chested, but Pope glowed, while Evans smoldered.

Les lounged in the forward bunk, bemused, mildly curious about this guy, but not challenged. Les had his own place of mind; he was self-contained. I was the odd man out, the man questing. Pope commanded my attention, provoked my spirit. Was he just another wild and crazy guy, another loose cannon, or was he the real thing, a Zen lunatic, a man living zestfully on the frontier of life?

That second fifth was soon almost gone, and so were Les and Bob Evans. But Pope, as I was to learn, never tipped over, although he always got drunk. The only apparent effect the booze had on him was to energize him further. It was fuel fed to the furnace in his breast. He had singled me out, sensing a kindred, or susceptible, spirit, a *paisano*, as he liked to put it. By the time we finished the fifth, we had told each other our stories.

He was from Ohio, his parents solid middle-class folks. But he had been in and out of trouble back there, at times a brilliant student, at times a juvenile delinquent, as they used to say. He was just sixteen when he ran away after some kind of nervous breakdown. He went straight to Alaska, but he didn't linger in the big city of Anchorage. It wasn't more civilization he was after. Somehow he hitched, walked, and bummed his way deep into the bush, striding forward with cocked shoulder and jutting chin, meeting all eventualities with bright eyes and a tight, gleeful grin. He wound up in the Iliamna country, where he met an Eskimo woman named Matrona, who was strong and capable in the woods. They built a cabin at the end of a maze of islands called Intricate Bay, straight across the lake from what was now the village of Iliamna, and they trapped and lived off the land and started having kids. Through Matrona's kinfolks he got into salmon fishing, at first in a marginal skiff but eventually swinging a deal with the cannery for a regular thirty-two-foot Bristol Bay gillnetter, which was now almost paid off.

Pope convinced us easily that night that it would be in our own best interest, regarding our wish to reach Dillingham and survive, to accept his offer to guide us. He was planning to start out for Dillingham himself in a couple of days. We were to follow him to his place on the lake, and we would leave together from there.

Between our present location and Dillingham lay not only the remaining fifty miles or so of Iliamna Lake, with its Jekyll and Hyde unpredictability, but another eighty miles of the equally shifty Kvichak River, which empties out of the lake and eventually flows into the salt water of Kvichak Bay. This river, Pope advised us solemnly, was not a simple highway to the sea. The big tides of Bristol Bay affect it in various ways, principally by varying its depth. In its middle portion, the river fractures into a myriad of channels, all looking to the uninitiated more or less plausible as the one to choose. All but one of them, however, were dead ends for anything drawing more water than a skiff, or they connected with the main channel only at the height of the biggest tides. A fish boat choosing the wrong channel on an ebb tide could easily be stuck for several weeks until another equally big tide reached it.

"Of course," Pope assured us, "you can always just go for it. You don't need me. Think of the adventure!"

He flashed his death's-head smile. And then there was this, too, he explained, that if we did happen to navigate the Kvichak successfully, we should not altogether trust our charts of the Naknek-Kvichak watershed, because the macho tides and bully waves were always pushing the sandbars around into unexpected places. Take Dead Man's Sands, for instance. We would of course have to skirt these on our way to Dillingham from Naknek. But, by God, it seemed that Dead Man's Sands had shifted some. It seemed they now stuck out so far you had to travel

halfway to Japan before it was safe to start rounding the corner
into Nushagak Bay—unless of course you knew the shortcut.
Pope knew the shortcut, but he didn't elaborate as to what it
was.

Gene Pope liked company, especially *cheechako* (Alaskan
slang for greenhorn) company smart enough to bring along a
case of booze. Also, the idea of a bona fide college professor
making this trip and wanting to be a fisherman and live in the
woods intrigued him. He sensed in me a friend and affirmation
of the adventure he had made his life.

One of the immediate consequences of my meeting Pope was
that sleep became something I used to get enough of and booze
something I got a lot more of, with the farther consequence that,
my chemistry and metabolism being radically altered, I entered
a most unordinary reality. (Everything is known in the mode of
the knower.) This new reality was like a poem by T. S. Eliot or
Dylan Thomas: vivid images dramatically juxtaposed but without rational order—a dream reality.

❖

The next morning the lake looked bad-tempered, hungover. The
waves, just beyond the islands, were black and frothing. The
wind blew cold and hard. Dark hairy clouds stalked along
the horizon. Pope's gillnetter, the *Otter*, was tough and seaworthy, broad-beamed and round-bottomed. Our slender *Port N
Storm* following behind the *Otter* looked like a lamb being led
to the slaughter. But none of that bothered me. I loved being
out on the lake in that weather (where ignorance is bliss). The
waves couldn't break more dashingly, the spray splash my face
more boldly. The boat was charged with the live power of the
lake, and it was like riding a bucking bronco in slow motion.

Then we were out of sight of the land, in every direction
only the lake and sky. I had no idea which way we were heading.
I knew we were following Pope to his place, but I couldn't

remember where he said it was, up the lake, down the lake, or across. The waves were big and bigger. At times, all we could see of the *Otter* were its exhaust pipe and antenna sticking out of the water. More than an hour went crashing by, and in all that chaos of wind and wave, the only thing for us to hang on to was the maroon shape of the *Otter* sporadically wallowing and disappearing ahead of us, with the grinning black figure at the wheel looking back and beckoning like the Pied Piper of doom.

Sometime after the third hour we caught sight of the solid rock mass called Tommy Point. It rose out of the waves like the forehead of a gigantic sperm whale. We passed behind its mass and were out of the reach of the waves and in among the islands of Intricate Bay. The bay was named Intricate because the islands large and small were scattered about haphazardly, like the pieces of an unsolved puzzle. There was no straight passage through but only a maze of twists and turns. Pope never slowed down. He zipped through narrow passages between sloping rock walls and spun brodies around the ends of islands. Some of the slots we slipped through were so small the *Otter* looked like an ocean liner.

"The son of a bitch is crazy," Les said out loud, but it was his inner thought.

No doubt about it. Pope was obviously mad. A late follower of the horned god—though he probably never heard of Dionysus, hiding out these days in the back regions of the world; suspect, subversive, marked for extinction, all remnants of the old consciousness, not just the animals and indigenous peoples, are being phased out by the abstracted mind of modern man. Gene Pope was obviously such a remnant, a marked man. Was he, for me, a saving remnant? Or a will-o'-the-wisp, an illusion partly of my own fabrication? Time would tell, perhaps, if I listened close enough. Meanwhile, the current of events had swept my life for better or worse into the turbulence of his wake. I was following close behind, ready or not.

And then we were there, at Pope-Vannoy landing, Pope's

place. In the dimming light, I made out a grass-covered bank and a dirt path leading to a couple of gray log cabins. In the smaller cabin lived Pope's uncle, Grant Vannoy, a reclusive gray-bearded bachelor who read strange books and engaged in long philosophical discussions with his intense and indefatigable nephew.

We cut the engines and tied up. The air was damp, sweet smelling, the land around obscure and still. I stood for a moment absorbing the silence and had a swift, uncanny sense of a living presence, that the land was aware and quietly breathing.

"See you guys in the morning," Pope flung the words over his shoulder as he jumped off the *Otter* and headed for his cabin. A group of small figures were clustered at the open door. Les and I stayed on board, glad to be relieved of any introductions. What we wanted was rest, a shot of sweet oblivion. I lay in my bunk, listening to the profound silence. It wasn't simply an absence of sounds but a positive, almost palpable presence, and again I felt it alive and breathing. But I was too tired to speculate and quickly fell asleep.

Then it was like twilight again. It could have been any of the early morning hours. I had no idea how long I'd slept, but I heard Pope's voice and the voices of kids, and laughter. Pope was coming down the path in his black boots and ragged jacket, his arm around the shoulders of a small woman, no doubt his wife Matrona. Four or five barefoot ragamuffins bounced along beside them carrying things for the *Otter*. Pope said his goodbyes laughing, bending down for hugs, then climbed on board. Little bigger than her small children, Matrona stood on the bank and waved to her husband heading for the fishing grounds, as Iliamna men had always done that time of year. Les and I stood ready. The engines thundered into life, and we glided away.

We moved out from among the islands under a cobalt sky with gray puffs of cloud, the clean blue waters now and then cresting white. After about an hour we passed offshore from a cluster of log and white-frame buildings lying just up from the gravel beach—Kakhonak, the only village on that side of the lake. The villagers were mostly Eskimo, with some white blood mixed in. Their lives were salmon fishing in the spring and summer; drying fish, hunting moose and caribou, gathering berries, and getting ready for winter in the fall; ice fishing and trapping in the winter—an ancient seasonal round. It seemed to me a good life, tied to the slow rhythms of the land. Yet even then many of the younger natives were as eager to enter the front door of the air-conditioned nightmare called the American dream as the variously disenchanted, such as I, were to get out the back.

Like Kakhonak, Igiugig, at the head of the Kvichak River, was a small village of mixed log and frame buildings. It lay scattered along the east bank above the river. Normally Pope would have stopped to visit, perhaps to party. But this time he went right on by. I think he wanted to have us and the considerable remnants of our case of whiskey to himself that night, and he planned on parking somewhere downriver. It certainly wasn't that he was in a hurry. Gene Pope didn't care if school kept or not, and he certainly never worried about being on time for anything, including making a living fishing in Bristol Bay.

There had been a while back on the lake when it had been calm enough for the two boats to run tied together. Pope had come aboard *Port N Storm*. He took special care at that time to instruct us about the fast rock-strewn stretches of the upper Kvichak, his eyebrows tilted upward in what I came to call Pope's serious and sincere look.

"The main thing," he said, "is when you follow me, stay close. And don't turn *when* I turn, turn *where* I turn." He was tight-lipped, suppressing his glee, watching our reactions, especially Les's. "In places the channel's only about half the width of the *Otter*." He let that sink in. Les shot me a look. "We will be moving with the current, which means we will be moving very fast." He paused again, savoring the occasion. "So what you have to do is make sure you can always see the whites of my eyes when I look back. Stay *that* close."

After we had untied the boats and Pope had pulled ahead, Les said, "I'm not sure I liked all that. I'm even less sure the bastard ain't just homicidal. As in 'homicidal maniac.' " There was some tension between the two Alaskans. Les was by nature careful: Look before you leap. And Pope was by determination careless: He who hesitates is lost—and also: The hairier the better.

Suddenly, we were into it, the Kvichak River. It felt like free fall, like being grabbed and taken by gravity.

"Holy shit!" said Les.

He rubbed the windshield rapidly with his sleeve, peering ahead. He was an experienced and able sailor, but this was something else. This was something he would have approached with prior consideration, if at all.

Pope, as usual, didn't slow down. To give him the benefit of the doubt in this instance, maybe he couldn't slow down and still maintain control, running with the current. Personally I would have tried descending that river in reverse.

Standing spread-legged at the wheel, Pope concentrated on the water ahead, leaning out to see better. Now and then he glanced back and flashed his demonic teeth.

So, I thought, this is what it's like hanging out with Captain Blood.

In the crystal water the boulders appeared mere inches below the surface, whizzing by like meteorites, and they were certainly real. This was not a Disneyland ride. The boulders wouldn't at the last split second disappear or turn into dancing girls.

"Oh, fuck!"

Les whipped the wheel hard to starboard. Too late. We ground to a jolting halt on a gravel bar, dug in hard. The current boiled against our listing starboard, the gunwale only inches above the foam. I hung on. What to do now? Jump overboard and push? Not a good idea. Even on the lee side of the boat the current would be too strong, would sweep the legs out from under a man. Les opened the hatch to see if we were taking on water. He slammed the cover and grabbed the long oar and tried pushing. I did the same with the boathook, leaning into it until the pole started to bend. The boat didn't budge.

I looked up and the *Otter* was coming back full bore against the current, churning up a big wave astern. Incredibly, in the narrow channel, Pope had managed to turn around.

"Throw you a line!" he yelled when abreast of us. His voice carried above the roar of the water as though through a bull-horn. Les moved up to the bow. Weaving in the current, Pope judged the distance, then, leaving the wheel, quick as a cat he grabbed the line draped over the center cleat, heaved it at us, and without breaking stride leaped back to the wheel, which had started spinning. The end loops of the line slapped our hull. Les grabbed for it and missed. When I looked, Pope was retrieving the line with one hand and holding the wheel with the other. He dropped back, playing the current. Then he was abreast again, a little closer this time, holding steady.

"All set?"

"Let her fly."

This time I didn't see Pope move, but here came the line, uncoiling straight at us. It whacked Les on the chest, and he grabbed it with both hands and quickly secured it to the cleat.

Wheeling in the current like a fighter plane peeling off, the *Otter* made a tight turn downstream, and the slack line came out of the water with a snap.

"Hold the wheel!" Les shouted. He grabbed the coping on the cabin. With a lurch and a horrible grating noise, in a haze of spray and at a crazy angle we were yanked off. I had sense enough left to hit the starter button. We straightened out downstream right behind the *Otter*. I goosed the engine to give Les the slack he needed to free the line. He jumped back down beside me.

"Jesus Christ," he said.

After that we followed behind the *Otter* not only close

enough to see the whites of Pope's eyes if he turned but close enough to read the leather label on his jeans if he didn't.

❀

An hour or so later the river slowed, broadened, and deepened. There was plenty of water under us now, no more boulders showing. We could relax. The *Otter* dropped back and we tied up together. Pope jumped aboard looking very serious.

"You know what I think?" he said. "I think that one calls for a *drink!*"

His laugh almost took my head off. We hadn't slept but a few hours, had almost swamped and who knows what else, and here came Pope looking like Mephistopheles at the slaughter of the innocents.

We swung about into the current and tied up to some stout alders along the cutbank. It was twilight again. We cut the engines. Coolness settled down with the silence. Above us the alders rustled in a wind that might have come off Arcturus. The river pushed past, speaking in tongues some part of me understood. Feeling once more the eerie presence of the land, I was glad to go below. We lit the light and the stove, broke out a jug, and entered our little human world.

We relived the day, much as men from earliest times have always done after an adventure, and what before had been anything but funny—not even Pope had been laughing when we were on the gravel bar—now seemed like a jolly good show worth rehearsing, and as we passed the bottle to one another we passed the buck of care onto that tomorrow that never comes.

"But you know," I said, just realizing the fact, "it all came and went so fast I don't think *I* had time to get scared—or maybe I didn't have sense enough to get scared. What do I know about getting hung up on gravel bars in Alaskan rivers?"

"Well, your clock must be running a hell of a lot faster than mine," said Les, "because I'm here to tell you *I* had time to get scared. That fucking current was *strong*. It would have swamped us sure, rolled us around like a log if the mad Captain Nemo here hadn't decided we could use a hand."

Pope's laughter, in those confined quarters, was something to be reckoned with. We poured another one all around, and I got my guitar and jumped right into the folk song about the hero young Monroe, who died breaking the jam on Jerry's rocks, and then I sang some sea chanteys and a song about the hard life of the old-time whalers.

> *A man must be blind*
> *To make up his mind*
> *To go to sea once more*

Pope had no trouble picking up on those songs. He couldn't get enough of them. They painted the picture in which he saw his own life. He also played and sang, about the wild gray goose and ladies left behind weeping, because his heart knows what the wild goose knows and he must go where the wild goose goes. His guitar playing was rough but strong, like his voice—kind of a cross between Nelson Eddy and the Righteous Brothers. And he wrote songs too, like this one about the fishing game:

> *Well the fishermen are fishing*
> *And we're sitting here just wishing*
> *That we'd float so we could go out fishing too*
> *But we won't sit and cry just because we're high and dry*
> *Because there's lots of booze and girls in town to screw*
>
> *Oh the radio is blaring*
> *And the fishermen are swearing*
> *Talking all about the fish they didn't get*
> *Why the hell should we listen*
> *When right now we can't go fishing*
> *And besides we think they're slightly full of shit*

We drank and sang until broad daylight peeked in and, as any decent broad would, invited us to come up and see her. So we went above and found the day to be fair indeed.

"What say, Professor," Pope declared, turning to me, brimming, "we head right on down, pick up my partner at Levelock, run on over to Naknek, and have us a *real* party."

Dispensing with so tedious a matter as sleep, in the exuberance of our meeting and under power of the booze, we cast off and headed down the Kvichak River, the two boats tied together. Les slept below on *Port N Storm*.

We stood in shirtsleeves, the day coming on clear and hot. The rolling land moved by tan and green, the air smelling sweet of it. Ducks rose up before us, and no doubt mink, beaver, otter, and maybe a wolf or two watched us pass. Some of the largest rainbow trout and arctic grayling in the world darted away at our approach.

Thoreau had written that there was a time in a man's life when he was apt to regard every likely spot as a possible site to build his home. I saw my cabin on the sunny rise of every bend, my skiff and kicker at the dock, the kids and I walking up the path with rainbows for breakfast, my wife calling from the porch, smoke from the cookstove rising out of the chimney.

In this country men were more involved with the land and animals than with people, if for no other reason than that there was so much of the former and so few of the latter. Lots of land and animals and weather and just a few people, all of them important. You didn't bounce around in a world full of strangers. It suited me: It had been the human experience shaping our species for maybe a million years. I believe human beings need a tight connection with the land and the weather and wild animals to be sane or whole. We need to know the earth is alive and sacred, the other animals our brothers and sisters, what indigenous peoples have always known. Concrete cubicles stacked on top of one another in concrete cities containing at best some pets and a zoo are a recipe for madness—though of course when

everyone around you is mad, who can tell the difference? To be
well-adjusted to an insane culture is to be insane.

❀

Levelock, near the mouth of the river on the west side, perched
over the eddying tide on the tall pilings of an abandoned cannery. After tying up, Les and I waited on the dock while Pope
went to get Edwin Peterson, his partner. The sprawling complex
of weathered wood and rusting metal buildings gave us our first
sense of the multimillion-dollar operation that salmon harvesting in Bristol Bay really was. This was not just the sideshow of
homesteaders and trappers making a few summer bucks fishing,
this was the big top of commercial salmon fishing—where our
gallant *Port N Storm* was destined to play the part of clown.

Gene Pope and Edwin Peterson coming toward us down the
plank corridor between cannery buildings fitted into this scene
in a way that not even Les did. Young men, both of them, they
nevertheless had the look of veterans, men who had been there
and back. Ed was about Gene's height, maybe five ten or so, but
of a slighter build. A native, he led the life, fishing in summer,
trapping in winter. He and Pope were building an airplane together, which they would share. They had been partners for
years, taking turns being captain. This was Pope's year to be
captain, and he didn't like it. He would rather let Ed make all
the tough decisions while he just cruised around on the sloop
*John B.*

Ed's eyes in his lean and fine-featured face were friendly and
without guile. He was clearly not into old-timer–cheechako
head games. He was straight on, a good-natured, genuinely
tough man. He smiled when we shook hands, and his teeth were
badly rotted.

❀

Out in Kvichak Bay heading for the cannery town of Naknek, we crashed through twelve-foot waves. It seemed to me we might just as well have been on an ocean instead of a bay. Those two gray-and-black figures ahead of us on the *Otter* didn't seem to notice. They were intent on going to town. I was intent on actually being there in Bristol Bay. And Les was intent on not losing sight of the *Otter*.

From the chart I knew we were threading our way through the maze of sandbars, running with the ebb. But the scene in front of me didn't look at all like the chart. The chart was clear-cut, numbered, and flat, whereas the scene in front of me looked like that time before time when the primal elements had yet to settle their differences. Some of the chaos out there could be brought home to my own head: operator problems, too much booze, too little sleep. Had I been sober and fully awake, it would all have come across differently, but I think it would have felt the same inwardly, only I wouldn't have known it.

Then as we approached the mouth of the Naknek River, which empties into the bay, we began seeing other boats a ways off, little fans of spray and splinters of color. When we reached the big bluffs at the broad entrance to the river, we passed among several huge black scows. They loomed above us like threshold guardians and seemed to be looking down on *Port N Storm* with a dry surmise. Fish boats and skiffs were anchored or darting about everywhere. There was excitement in the air. It was twilight again, and the mast lights crackling white and the red and green running lights bobbing and streaking up, down, and across gave the river the look of a frenetic pinball machine. Flat scows and blunt-faced tenders moored in the powerful current pulled at their lines like tethered bulls foaming at the mouth, and the smaller boats at anchor appeared to be plunging ahead, curling the water to either side. Many more boats upstream, where it was calmer, were tied in rows off one or another of the cannery docks lining the river. The town itself, a cluster of small houses, stood above the fray on the bluff. Its lights seemed to wink and pulse in concert with the sparklers below.

We tied up together, with the *Otter*'s anchor out, just off from one of the docks whose black pilings rose above us like a petrified forest. The air smelled of mud and fish and was loud with the cries of seagulls.

I was now what is called spacey. Pope hopped on board bright-eyed and bushy-tailed as ever. Apparently he got all the sleep he needed for the summer through the winter of long nights, storing it as a camel stores water. I couldn't see straight, and when I grinned at him it felt as if only one side of my mouth was working. He roared at my expression, and Ed, whose head was sticking into the cabin, smiled broadly, unconscious of his black teeth. They were going somewhere. Hang tough, Professor. Stay awake, VanDevere. They would be back pronto. There would be girls. Tundra bunnies! Somewhere, they had gotten a tippy little rowboat. They disappeared into the shadows under the pilings.

"Jesus Christ," said Les. "How does that guy do it?" He collapsed on his bunk and in a matter of seconds had died with his boots on and was snoring. I stretched out on my own cozy little bunk, feeling the motion of the boat, smelling the strange air of Naknek. I suppose I passed out of the picture or just wandered off in my head, because next I was aware of voices and oars splashing, then a bump and Pope's voice outside a couple of feet from my head.

"Hey, Professor! Don't crap out on us now. Come on over and meet Janet and Claire. VanDevere! Let go your cock and grab your sock. These bunnies are dying to meet you!"

Les roused, sat up. I called back, "Yeah, okay, Gene. Give me a minute till I wake up." It was dark inside as well as outside my head. Les stumbled about, searching for his cap.

"You coming, Bob? Come on. What the hell, this whole thing's screwy anyway."

"Yeah, okay, Les. You go ahead. I've got to get my shit together a little before I can move."

I heard him go for another jug, the glass clinking, and he went up on deck. *Port N Storm* rocked lightly as he stepped over onto the *Otter*.

I had this one sweet corner of darkness all to myself. I was mildly and briefly tempted to join them, see what happened if I went all the way. Morality was a thing of the past, part of the old life. For a while, on and off, I heard laughter, and some time or other Pope playing guitar and singing. I was somewhere else, someone else. All parameters were obviated. Then I was slowly coming up out of it, because a female voice, hoarse and angry, was shouting: "You dirty rotten bastards!" Something, a frying pan or pot, banged and clattered. More cursing and screaming, glass breaking, and male voices in a jumble, perhaps angry. The boats rocked. There was a big splash and confused shouting. But the bunk was warm and snug, my body committed to it like an iron filing to a magnet. I really didn't care one way or the other. It was their problem, let them handle it. I was on the deep.

❂

Sometime in the morning, I didn't really know when—I had lost track of time in the perpetual daylight-twilight of Bristol Bay's June—we were under way again, the river hectic with boats and skiffs, the drone of their engines filling the air. We nudged into the gas dock, banging against the other boats crowding in. More confusion. Hungover and spaced out. Handling the wet lines, the icy gas nozzle. The strong smell of fumes. Pope, hands on hips, leaning back grinning insanely up at some guy in a gray shirt and white cap leaning over the dock talking to him. The river, even way up by the gas dock, choppy, knocking the boats against one another. On the bluff, silver sheets of saw grass rippling, snapping in the wind. Steel-wool clouds scudding low across the hunched land. What must it be like outside?

We were striking out for the Nushagak on this tide. *Port N Storm* would be following the *Otter*. I had studied the charts. On the ebb a boat must keep to the channels down the Naknek-Kvichak watershed, then virtually head out to sea in order to escape the long reach of Dead Man's Sands, and then make a wide, slow right turn, still way out to sea, to stay clear of the broad shoals and hit the east or middle channel of Nushagak Bay.

Old-time bush pilots flew by the seat of their pants. Gene Pope navigated by dead reckoning. He looked the territory over. But beside Johnson Hill, about halfway down Kvichak Bay, there was nothing to see but everything the same: the sea, the sky, the vagrant thin line of land. The least bit of fog or just the twilight could obliterate all distinctions. Yet Pope knew where he was. Or if he didn't always know, he nevertheless proceeded as if he did. He operated under the assumption that he could get out of any trouble he could get into. Living life as an adventure, which was his predilection, probably required that kind of faith, though that kind of faith is blind.

It must have been in the spirit of adventure, and with a ballast of ignorance, that Les and I followed Pope out of the shelter of the Naknek River. As the mouth of the river widened past the bluffs, merging with the bay, the wind intensified. It looked grim out there. The waves were doing the Watusi, getting really worked up, jabbing at the low-flying clouds. Pope's broad-shouldered gillnetter smashed its way through, hurling the waves to either side in tumults of foam. But it seemed likely our little misfit lady *Port N Storm* would be getting in way over her head, so to speak. Her name suited her capabilities: In a storm, head for port, not open sea.

After about fifteen minutes following the *Otter*, the constant pounding apparently succeeded in jolting Les out of the trance

Naknek and the previous night's debauch had put him in. "Fuck this," he said and cut the throttle. We swung idly about, wallowing in the seas like a dead seal. But the seas didn't accept our capitulation. The first big broadside wave, wanting in, tipped us down to the gunwale, dousing us with heavy spray. I heard things bouncing around below in the cabin. Les throttled back up to where he could hold the bow into the waves, waiting to see what Pope would do if he noticed us dropping behind.

The *Otter* was turning, coming back. Just within shouting range, Pope swung out along the gunwale onto the bow. His shirt was open at the neck, sleeves rolled to the elbow. He wore no hat. Les and I were in rain gear, sou'westers and all. Somehow Pope stood there, hands on hips, now above, now below us, the diffused sheen of the ragged sun behind him making of his form a blurred silhouette that appeared, when a wave raised him aloft, larger than life, like a visitation, angelic or demonic.

"You guys conked out already?" he called across, his big voice easily bridging the gap.

"Too rough for *Port N Storm*, Gene," Les shouted back. His tone was matter-of-fact, but I knew he was uneasy about the situation. "We're gonna wait for a better day, maybe follow behind a scow."

Pope stared at us in disbelief. Edwin nudged the *Otter* closer. "Too rough! Shit, man, this is just two degrees shy of flat calm in Bristol Bay. You could grow old waiting for a better day." He looked directly at me, figuring no doubt that since it was my boat I must be the captain, but I had deferred to Les's experience. "What say, Professor? Now or never's the name of the game. Hell, we'll throw you a line and *tow* you over!"

He stood there on the bow of the plunging boat like a bareback rider in a circus. His black hair whipped about, and his shirttails cracked in the wind. Pope didn't say the words, but I understood his meaning. Was I in earnest about living in the bush and fishing for a living, or was I just another armchair adventurer, a fair-weather sailor? Pope was too much. I had to believe in him. I used to believe in Errol Flynn when I was a kid, but here was Pope—no music in the background, unless you counted the wind whistling across the exhaust pipe—real and in person and looking right at me.

"Let's go for it, Les," I said.

VanDevere glanced at me from under his cap. He looked absolutely disgusted, seemed about to protest, but just swore softly and reached for the throttle. He was between the rock of his better judgment and the hard place of his pride. "Better get ready to catch that fucking line, just for starters," he said to me, turning away. He swung the bow around in line with the *Otter*.

"Hey! All right!" Pope laughed. "No sweat, man!"

Edwin turned the *Otter*'s stern to us, and Pope moved lightly from the bow to the stern, like a tightrope walker without a safety net (one missed step and over he goes), a coiled line crooked in his arm. I hopped up onto the wet gunwale, gripping the piping on the cabin, and made my way as casually as possible up to the bow (one missed step and over I go). But as the poet said, if the sun and moon should doubt, they'd immediately go out. I didn't doubt for a moment that I was indestructible. Some part of my mind recognized the possibility of falling overboard and drowning, of course, but the rest of me, the majority, was utterly without concern. The ambition or need that drove me to this gamble had long ago accepted the life-or-death stakes.

I stood on the bow with my legs as far apart as possible, feet braced against the raised edge, riding the boat as the boat rode the waves. Pope made his cast, and the line uncoiled in slow motion, coming right at me. I caught the last fathom against my chest, took a quick bite on the cleat, and cinched it down. Pope waved thumbs up and slipped back to the wheelhouse. Edwin, a Bristol Bay fisherman all his life, had watched the entire maneuver as one might watch a neighbor mow the lawn.

As the *Otter* moved out, she was simultaneously lifted by a big wave, and the towline sprang taut as an electrocuted eel. We lurched forward. Les hit the throttle.

"Better hang on!" He looked at me with a peculiar wan smile. "This could be a rough ride, Professor."

I was hanging on, in boots, slicker, and sou'wester, with both hands. We rode up some waves and dived through others, the *Otter* disappearing in the spray, and more than spray, solid waves that struck with force, obliterating the world. Then, as the windshield cleared, the two gray and black figures on the *Otter* would reassemble, looking, through the wet glass, like a pointillist painting.

Les and I took turns at the wheel and at the hand bilge pump in the stern. Getting astern, with the boat lunging and bucking like a Brahma bull, and with the haphazard jerk of the towline confounding things, was an adventure in itself. Hands and knees was the only way to go, and even so I got knocked around and skinned my shins. If the *Otter* hadn't been breaking trail for us, our little homemade lady might have taken more of a beating than she could survive.

"Take the wheel a minute," Les said in a neutral tone after maybe an hour or so, not looking at me. "I want to check on something."

He went below, and when he came back up he wore that peculiar glinty-eyed smile again. "According to what I see on the chart and our position with Johnson Hill, we're way too far over on the west side. You know what I think?" He took out his handkerchief and wiped his glasses, still not looking at me. "I think we're heading right down the Dead Man's throat."

Uh oh, uh oh. Dead Man's Sands were not so named without cause. I studied Les's face for a moment: Was he putting me on? He continued wiping his glasses, his face impassive. I peered ahead. The water did look really mean up a ways, but then it had looked mean all along.

"There." Les pointed off the starboard bow. Surf was breaking along a stretch of exposed sand. It reminded me of Rockaway Beach on the Atlantic Ocean. The breakers were yellow instead of gray-green and white, but they were of similar caliber. Surf was breaking further out off the port bow too. Apparently, we were heading into a channel of sorts, a narrow chute between the lines of breakers.

*Port N Storm* had no Fathometer, so we couldn't know how much water we had under us. Neither, I recalled, did the *Otter* have a Fathometer, although it's considered essential equipment on a fish boat. So Pope was indeed proceeding by dead reckoning (apt phrase)—taking a shortcut across Dead Man's Sands.

Les stood tight-lipped at the wheel, trying to think of a way out but seeing none. Were we to cut loose and try for the deep-water channel on the east side we would most likely wind up adorning one or another of the Dead Man's fingers of sand. Les shook his head. Now he looked at me. "The bastard's not just crazy. He's criminally insane." He spoke matter-of-factly. No point getting worked up now. We were in the chute and would have to run the gauntlet as best we could.

"If we survive, or either one of us, we should sue the son of a bitch," he continued, really at the moment quite in earnest. "He can afford to bounce off the bottom now and then, feeling his way through. That's a commercial hull, built to take a lot of shit. *Port N Storm* will crack open like an egg."

With Les and me the spilled yolk, food for fishes.

*I'm in the deep*
*I'm fast asleep*
*The fishes watch me round*

What would they tell my kids? "Full fathom five thy father lies; . . . Those are pearls that were his eyes." I wished we had five fathoms under us now. We would have been much less likely to suffer that sea change into something rich and strange.

But here we were, breakers to the right of us, breakers to the left of us, and there was nothing we could do but lower our lances and charge.

As the windshield cleared, I noticed Pope looking back at us deliberately. When he caught my eye, he frowned darkly and pointed off to the right at the exposed bar and breakers. Then he turned to the port side and let his mouth drop open, smacked his forehead with his palm, and staggered backward. The breakers on that side were very close. The next green one hit our windshield and wiped away the sight of Pope himself breaking into a big laugh. I could almost hear him above the volleying and thundering.

Les took it all in with a straight face: A lot of it was no doubt meant for him. Suddenly he leaned forward into the windshield and yelled at the top of his voice. "You fucking crazy bastard!" But then he broke into a laugh despite himself. He pulled his cap down over an eye and looked at me. "And are you enjoying the ride, Professor?"

As a matter of fact, in some weird way, yes I was. I felt no anxiety at all at the time. I felt in fact an urge to jump into an old-time sailor's jig right there on the deck. Instead, I leaned way out and shook my fist at Pope, getting drenched, salt water in my mouth.

Pope roared and did break into a kind of jig, and Les seemed oddly cocky, grinning over at me from under his cap. It wasn't the booze anymore; it was the trip and, probably, the danger we were helpless to avoid. What the hell. Throw the reins down on the horse's neck and enjoy the ride. Nobody lives forever. We owe God a death, as the great bard put it, and he who pays today is quits for tomorrow. Everything for the past several days had been a little askew, a little surreal, anyway. Certainly, we were focused exclusively on the present moment. No dithering of consciousness now, no daydreaming of the past, no imagining the future. Here and now, boys, here and now. Maybe Pope wasn't a madman after all. Maybe he was a Zen gift, a knock on the head at just the right time. God, as they say in Tierra del Fuego, works in mysterious ways.

Lack of sleep or even rest had something to do with it. Earlier, I had tried going below and lying on my bunk. *Port N Storm*'s flat bottom came down so hard I thought my spine might snap, and I did whack my head on a shelf. Forget about rest; we didn't need it. We had shifted into overdrive. Still, I wished we had established firmer communications with Pope before we started out: "No shortcuts through Dead Man's Sands, Pope, or we and our booze wait till we can sneak across behind a scow."

And then we were through, the sands behind us. No more surf. Just the generally madcap sea and pell-mell sky. We looked back to where we had just been, and the surf there was still up, even more sand showing as the tide ebbed. But had the shortcut really been less of a threat than we had supposed? Had Pope been having fun at our expense? (I later learned that almost no one attempted that route, which is some indication of the hazards involved. And those sands were not named Dead Man's in jest. Many brave hearts lie asleep in the deep.)

The sands were behind us, but the rest of the trip was before us, and Les and I were still very much at sea. Now that we had passed Johnson Hill, we saw only water. We knew the land lay off our starboard side somewhere, but it was lying low, nothing but a long, broad shoal we had to skirt in making the slow curve around Etolin Point and into Nushagak Bay. We settled down to toughing out the hours, about a ten-hour run from Naknek to Dillingham. The trick was to time it right, ride the ebb out from Naknek and catch the flood into the Nushagak. Otherwise you bucked tide, which could mean a very long haul, because the tides in Bristol Bay are big and strong.

Then we caught sight of something ahead, recognizable in a minute as a bell-shaped buoy lolling heavily about. "That's probably one of the outside marker buoys," Les said, "marking the outside limit to the Nushagak fishing grounds. We must be into the Nushagak, off Etolin Point." He patted the wheel. "So far, so good, for the good ship *Port N Storm*." Yes, our little jewel was making it in the Big Apple of salmon-fishing waters. She had lost her innocence, to be sure, but not her life, so far.

❀

We were moving up the middle channel of Nushagak Bay with the flood. The clouds had thinned and broken up, the wind had eased off, and the water had calmed appreciably. The evening was spread out across an endless sky, vistas fanning out before us. Everything appeared as though seen through a wide-angle lens. The land in the distance lay mute and flat, treeless, a few hills far off resembling the breasts of a woman lying on her back, the sky behind them a luminous strip of orange and red brooded over by purple clouds. It seemed almost overdone, Hollywood, except that the wind in my ear didn't speak of a celluloid civilization. This wind whispered of subatomic spaces and interstellar silences. This was not Hollywood. Nature here wasn't backdrop to some exclusively human drama occupying center stage. In the face of this stark land the strutting of some big man could be seen as no more than ludicrous. This country wrote its own script and followed no direction but its own. You couldn't cage it in your old ideas and images, pin it fixed to the wall of your mind. Categories like "picturesque" and "magnificent" couldn't contain it. Such concepts could only get in the way of what was there before you—the thing itself, the inscrutable land itself, mysterious and powerful.

Soon we began to see lights up ahead in the dusk, white sparkles thick as stars. We came on them first in groups of twos and threes and then in denser clusters: the mast lights of boats and scows at anchor, waiting off Clarks Point for the fishing to start at the designated hour. Hundreds of boats, most of them with their cabin lights glowing and here and there winding among them the red and green running lights of boats under way. The fleet looked like a city seen from the air at night. We knew at once that this was big time. Everything about Bristol Bay was bigger and more imposing than either of us could have imagined. It had that kind of strong presence that startles you into attention, so that you see it as with a child's new eyes: an opening, a rift in the familiar world letting a little wonder in.

As we neared Dillingham we saw other groups of lights on a bluff to the west, and up ahead the lights of the town itself looked like another flotilla. The cannery buildings and docks directly fronted our approach. Behind them the town rose on a gentle hill overlooking the bay.

A big tender, broad and blunt-ended, and a couple of dozen fish boats and skiffs lay together tied in rows off the dock pilings. The tide was high, and the air smelled of the sea and was cold. We moved in slowly to tie up to the *Otter*. Pope was talking to some guys on another boat. I stood ready on the bow with the coiled line in my hand.

# 3

# OUR FIRST SEASON FISHING

Because we didn't know anyone beside Gene Pope and Edwin Peterson, both of whom had disappeared into Dillingham, Les and I spent the next couple of days getting ready to fish. No one was coming around inviting us to go for a beer, so we were sober and diligent. We didn't realize yet that as a couple of outsider white guys we would not be warmly welcomed by native Alaskan fishermen.

The first order of business was to get our nets on board. Les had air-freighted them over from Kenai, and they were hanging somewhere in the net loft among dozens of others. The loft was large, airy, and amber, constructed of spruce, with heavy hewn beams from which the nets hung. It smelled of hemp and tar, although those materials weren't much used anymore. Charlie, the net boss, an old Eskimo, sat in the sun by one of the large multipaned windows placidly tying new nylon webbing onto a corkline, his hands moving rapidly in an easy rhythm. He looked up as we approached, and when we told him what we were after he indicated with his head where our nets should be, observing us closely, since we were new hands. He said nothing and kept on working.

The length of each net, or shackle, was fifty fathoms, or three hundred feet, with a string of floats, the corkline, along the top edge and a lead line along the bottom, properly weighted to keep the webbing stretched between the two. In former days the floats had been made of wood and the lead line of hemp with lead weights pinched on. Now the floats were lightweight Styrofoam, and the lead ran through the center of the rope, thus eliminating the lead knobs, on which the webbing had always gotten hung up. The substitution of Styrofoam for wood along the corkline helped lighten the nets, but they were still heavy.

Hung from their middles, with the cork and lead lines tied into separate bundles, the nets looked like upside-down bouquets. After they were lowered to the floor, one man swung the congregated corks over his shoulder, and the other hoisted the bunched lead line over a shoulder, the webbing hanging between them. The cork end was bulky, but the lead end was heavy. The first time I swung the leads over my shoulder, with a great macho effort, the pendulum of their weight carried me off my feet and into a pile of old nets. Les helped me up, grinning. "I did that, too, the first time," he said. Charlie looked up with a straight face and kept on sewing, much too considerate to laugh. At the next try I managed to stay on my feet, and we started out into the bright sunlight with the first net slung between us. With each step the bunched lead line hanging down my back swung heavily from side to side, but not in synchronization with my stride, and I staggered along behind Les like a drunken sailor. With the next two nets, I grabbed the corkline. Les was bigger than I.

We laid the nets on the dock above where *Port N Storm* was tied off the pilings. The tide was out, and the boat was about twenty feet down. Les descended the ladder and stood on the lower afterdeck by the roller, while I undid the ties and lowered him a net. He coiled the cork and lead lines into separate piles as they came, first tying a bowline loop in the "bridle" (the fathom of line without corks on each end of the net) of the first net down and looped it over a stern cleat, so that when the three connected nets were laid out to fish they would be attached to the boat. On the end of the last shackle let down, which would be the first to go out over the roller, Les tied (again with the bowline) the big orange buoy with our ADF&G (Alaska Department of Fish and Game) number on it. The buoy not only identified the nets but, especially in rough water, was indispensable for keeping tabs on where the end of your nets were in relation to the other nets and boats around. Then, too, when threading your way through a body of water crisscrossed with nets, the big brightly colored end buoys were what you looked for. You see the boat at one end and spot the buoy at the other. Then you know where their nets are and can dodge around them.

In nasty weather and at night it can get very tricky. You have to keep sharp watch, because if you accidentally run over someone's corkline, the chances are good that it will wrap your propeller despite the metal baskets most boats have around their props. When this happens, you wish it hadn't. Your boat is stopped dead, you are caught in the net. One way or another, you will have to free yourself from the corkline and webbing wrapped around your propeller. If your bad luck turns good, reversing the engine could free you, but if your bad luck stays that way more drastic measures will have to be tried—like tying a line around your middle (fixed to a cleat) and going over the side with a sharp knife and a deep breath. Many of the newer commercial hulls have a removable brass plate about the circumference of a man's arm in the deck just above the propeller, so that only an arm need go into the frigid water to cut the net free. (Before unscrewing such a plate you want to be sure the bilge pump is in working order.)

With the nets coiled in the stern, the gas tank full, the water and grub on board, Les and I were ready to go fishing. The salmon generally appear each year with remarkable consistency of timing, but they don't come all at once. In Bristol Bay the kings (chinook salmon) arrive first, and many fishermen own king gear—nets with the legal-size mesh for the big fish—and they will be out there fishing when the air, as well as the water, is just thawing out after the long winter. As the king run dwindles, the first considerable numbers of reds (sockeye salmon) gradually appear. Early fishing for reds, before the bulk of the pack arrives (the Big Run) is known as "scratching." Many fishermen, especially the outside fishermen, arrive just before the Big Run and quit directly afterward, actually fishing for a period of only a couple of weeks or so. They reap the greatest monetary reward for the least expenditure of time. But local and especially native fishermen tend to do a little scratching before and after the Big Run, even if they don't go after the kings. They like to fish, and they like the slower pace and uncrowded conditions of scratch fishing. Les and I had the itch to fish, so for us a little scratching was in order.

❁

When the tide was right one sunny morning, just ebbing good, we set about heading for the fishing grounds. I say "set about" because there was more to getting clear of the dock than just starting the engine and going. *Port N Storm* was one of several boats tied in parallel off the pilings. Dwarfed by the boats on either side, she was the obvious oddball. We wished to exit with as much correctness and dignity as possible. With Les at the wheel, first I undid the stern lines connecting us to the other boats. But of course I couldn't allow the sterns of the three outside boats abreast of us to drift away disconnected while their crews slept or were ashore. So I took the stern line of the adjacent outside boat, to which the others were tied, and stretched it across *Port N Storm* to the stern cleat of the boat inside us, thus reconnecting it to the dock via the other boats parked parallel. Then I scrambled up to the bow and undid those lines. I held onto the outside neighbor's bowline and worked my way astern as Les moved *Port N Storm* forward out of her slip. When our stern was abreast of the other boats' bows, I hopped onto the inside boat's gunwale with the outside boat's bowline, pulled the three outside boats in, and quickly cinched the line down. Then I slipped back to the stern and, using all my strength, managed to pull their ass ends in snug. Darting back to the bow of the inside boat, while Les held *Port N Storm* steady against the tide, I then jumped back down onto our stern deck. Nothing to it!

But getting out of a crowd of boats wasn't always that involved. Usually there was someone aboard one or another of the adjacent boats who would help handle the lines. But Alaska has a way, according to my superstition, of testing newcomers hard right off, setting up worst-case scenarios at the start. Maybe the Big Eskimo in the Sky just wants to let you know right away what you're letting yourself in for, so that you can disengage yourself from the Great Land before you're in too far to back out. It's as though the land were trying to warn you: *I'm not quite so romantic as you might have imagined as you watched your hero strutting nowth to Alaskah across the comfortable silver screen.*

The day was fair, the wind fresh, and the high spirits of their interplay teased the water into a display of white smiles. *Port N Storm* seemed to catch the mood. She skipped from wave to wave like a young girl at hopscotch. Her engine hummed along, and her sharp green bow sliced the waves to either side in arcing curves that frothed away clean and bubbly.

Up ahead the white cannery buildings of Clarks Point gleamed on a low green bluff. A couple of dozen fish boats and a scow rode at anchor in the protection of the point. Beyond, the bay widened into open water. Here and there other boats were already laid out and fishing, the white lines of their nets snaking out to the big red end buoys standing out against the sienna water.

For Les and me it was just a guess as to where we should try. We didn't know where the fish hung out or what avenues they might travel on their way home. That took years of experience or some friendly advice, and we had neither. So we randomly picked a nice open spot away from the boats but in the general vicinity, hoping to snag a few strays anyway. We had no great expectations, we were just testing the water and ourselves.

We were ready to lay out for the first time. Les stood by the wheel, while I went astern. He swung *Port N Storm* around with the wind astern and cut the engine to an idle, letting the wind push us forward at about the right speed. Had there been no wind, he would have used the engine to maintain headway so that the nets would uncoil and play out over the roller as we moved ahead. I heaved the lead line and the end buoy, tied to the corkline, over our makeshift roller. But I didn't put quite enough heave into it, and the buoy and lead line hung just short of the water, looking ridiculous.

Les laughed good-naturedly. "Feed some more of the lead and corklines over," he said.

Which I did, and when the buoy hit the water as I continued feeding the lines over the roller, the waves grabbed the buoy and net and ran with them. *Port N Storm* had become a sailboat pushed smartly by the wind, and the nets uncoiled properly and rattled over the roller and into the water, and we were fishing.

Fishing is like hunting. As hunting isn't necessarily finding, fishing isn't necessarily catching. We had heard that some boats were delivering fifty to one hundred salmon a day, but we were ready to consider this a dry run—or, more exactly, what is called a "water haul": pulling the nets back into the boat with nothing but water clinging to them. A practice session.

Only the first shackle was out, and already the end buoy seemed surprisingly far away. I watched the second shackle stringing out, making sure there were no kinks in it. Suddenly our first fish hit, close to the boat. There was no mistaking it, even though the hit was low and didn't produce a splash. About half a dozen corks shivered and bowed out from the line.

"There's a hit!" yelled my usually restrained partner.

Then three more fish plowed into the webbing near the cork-line, raising geysers of spray. I got excited and almost caught a foot in the net still feeding out over the roller. I shot a glance back at Les and could see that, even after ten years of fishing, he was as hyped as I was about these first hits. Apparently men don't get jaded about catching fish any more than they do about trying to catch women. Both pursuits have an ancient lineage and a tireless fascination.

When we quit for the day, we had fifty-six brilliantly irides-cent, hard-bodied sockeye salmon in our hold. With the nets neatly re-coiled in the stern, we headed back up the bay. Several other boats were heading in with their catches, too, silhouetted against the long amber evening. My boots and rain gear were spattered with slime and scales, and I felt as if I had been anointed. I had gone fishing in Bristol Bay and had caught salmon and we were part of the fleet and I was a fisherman. No matter that neither I nor my boat looked the part. *Port N Storm* looked like she belonged on a freshwater lake and I looked like I belonged in a duck blind. My tan parka and brown hip boots were right out of Eddie Bauer, replete with all the buckles and buttons intrinsic to such gear—buckles and buttons the nylon webbing found irresistible. I spent as much time extricating my-self as I did extricating the fish. A gillnetter's slicker and boots are black, heavy gauge, and devoid of buckles, straps, and but-tons. I would have to purchase regulation gear before we went out again.

We headed for a scow off Clarks Point to deliver our fish to them. I grabbed my peughstick—a kind of broom handle with a sharp curved metal point with which to stick the fish in the head and "shovel" them into the brailer, the big net with rope-size webbing that the scow lowers into the hold of the delivering boat and when full lifts to empty the catch into its own hold.

The hands on the tally scow to whom we delivered our fish didn't seem to notice my oddball appearance or my misfit boat. Nor did they snicker or pause in their tallying when a few of the fish I heaved at the brailer slipped off my peughstick and landed back in the water. They might have enjoyed a joke or two at my expense that night around the mess table, but they showed no sign of mirth as they tallied our catch and duly registered it in our fish book, and as far I was concerned I was a commercial harvester.

After delivering we anchored among a bunch of other boats off Clarks Point and washed *Port N Storm* down with buckets of salt water, cleaned ourselves up the same way, and were ready for supper, feeling not only good but triumphant. It was a tradition among salmon fishermen in Alaska to keep the first fish over the roller to eat. I wondered if maybe this practice wasn't a remnant of our kind's primal regard for the fish, as for all wildlife taken, as a gift bestowed by, let's say, the Great Mystery, their lives given sacramentally to sustain ours. To most fishermen today the fish means only money: They see dollar bills coming over the roller. But dimly, in this tradition, maybe they see the fish otherwise, too, in the old way.

❀

Living on board that first season was fun (for the most part), something like camping out, life simplified, reduced to a few essentials, with no room for a lot of *stuff*. The two-burner propane stove heated the little cabin quickly on rainy days, and it was positively luxurious lying at anchor being gently rocked by the water at night in my snug bunk, warm and dry, listening to the soft patter of raindrops overhead. And on sunny days during closed periods (when no fishing was permitted), before we got plugged into D Inn Crowd, Les and I worked in our T-shirts mending net or beefing up a stern cleat. Or trying to plug leaks sprung in *Port N Storm*'s cabin structure by the battering we got in rough weather, bashing against the steel hulls of the scows as we delivered. Rainy nights weren't so luxurious when little rivulets of cold water found their way into our bags, and new cracks were always opening up. *Port N Storm* hadn't been reared to take the hard knocks of commercial salmon fishing. She had been a suburban playgirl who had endured no abuse harsher than an occasional bumpy landing at the lakefront dock.

But leaks could be the least of a man's discomforts living at the cannery dock. For one thing, the air could become ripe with the odor of fishheads and entrails when the tide was out and the sun was too. The cannery dumped its waste directly into the water or mud beneath the dock, and it was a smell you didn't get used to, that didn't white out. Fortunately, however, the tides were a dependable sanitation department; they arrived on time and made a clean sweep of things. For another thing, when the tide was in, the motion of the water wasn't uniformly gentle and soothing. Sometimes the wind blew hard directly up the bay, right at the dock area, and the boats tied together off the pilings became a kind of conga line, especially if, as was usually the case, the lines between a few of the boats were a little slack. Hard lurches would be followed by hard bumps, in unremitting succession. A man had to be very tired or drunk to sleep through that.

Occasionally, most often in the middle of the night when it was not only blowing but raining, it got too rough to ride it out by the dock. On such a night early in the season, I was awakened by the boats jerking and banging against one another. I lay there not knowing what to expect or do. Les was still asleep. Pretty soon I heard loud voices, and an engine started, then others. Someone jumped down on *Port N Storm* just over our heads. "Gotta move out, you guys," a voice called. I sprang out of my bunk and scrambled up on deck, Les pulling on his pants behind me. The guy from the boat tied to us on the inside was undoing the bowline. They were getting away from the dock: too rough. I hopped up onto our bow, barefoot and in my underwear, grabbed our bowline and jumped with it onto the bow of the boat that wanted to leave, and then onto the next boat in, as the departing boat puller tossed Les the stern line of the inside boat as his bow passed our stern, and Les then pulled our ass end in.

I jumped back on board, wet and shivering now, my bare feet cold as ice. The rain stung like hail. Other boats were starting up, and some fellows were coming down the ladders to move their boats, their slickers wet and shiny and flapping in the wind.

"We better get out of here, too, I guess," Les said.

We got into our rain gear, not even bothering to change underwear. Everyone was moving out now. Our wool long johns, although wet, would hold enough heat in. "Vear da vool, vear da vool," counseled the archetypal Swede, "and no matter how cold and vet you get you'll alvays be varm and dry."

Everyone was heading for the small-boat harbor, about half a mile west of the docks. In the semidarkness, we followed the other boats' running lights. The channel into the harbor was narrow and, in the dim light, tricky. You could get stuck in the mud. Certainly *we* could.

Inside the harbor basin, a chaos of boats were jockeying around to find a spot, engines revving, men shouting. Too many boats, too few spaces. After a lot of milling around and bumping other boats, we saw a narrow slot next to a big skiff and squeezed into it, happy for once about *Port N Storm*'s narrow beam. The hubbub all around continued for about an hour, then gradually abated. All the boats were in except those whose crews were uptown and unaware of the blow. These boats would take a beating at the dock until the tide went back out and left them settled quietly in the mud. By now it had gotten fairly light. We lit the stove and got out of our rain gear and wet underwear and into some dry clothes. We started feeling pretty good. Everything is known by its contrary, philosophers say—light by dark, heat by cold, pleasure by pain. I was to find the fisherman's life, and Alaska, full of those kinds of strong contraries. We were on the up side of some that morning.

❖

A stormy night wasn't required, however, for a man's rest to be disturbed. A neighbor could decide he had to go somewhere at any time, and even if you didn't have to pile out of the sack, there would be a lot of noise and thumping about overhead. Or a couple of late boozers might jump, heavily, from boat to boat on their way to their own. Inasmuch as *Port N Storm* sat a couple of feet lower than the other boats, the jump involved would be not only across but down. Les slept up forward, under the bow. The first guy landing a foot above his head would burst upon his dreams like the crack of doom and the second like a call to arms.

Then, too, there was always the possibility that a belligerent drunk might clamber on board for something when you were all zipped up in your bag. Which happened once during a long closed period in 1967 when I was partners with Gene Pope. Our boat was parked up on the dock for repairs, resting on wooden blocks placed under the keel. She was snug up against a cannery building, safe and sound above the reach of wind and tide. A good place to catch up on sleep, especially since Pope was up-town some place for the night.

After a mild evening in town—just a few drinks and a laugh or two—I strolled down the deserted dock in the half-light of Bristol Bay's midnight. The air was cool and smelled of the sea. Except for the gulls off the end of the dock, it was quiet. Even the cannery machinery observed the strange quietus of sleep. No matter how frantic the day and its ambitions, everyone and everything, on this night at least, seemed to be resting in the unconscious understanding that, after all, it doesn't matter.

I borrowed a short ladder leaning against another boat nearby and climbed on board, wondering what I might find for a little snack as I felt around in my pocket for the key to the cabin door. There was a damp chill in the air, and since I was pre-paring for a luxurious night's rest, I lit a burner. While the cabin was warming, I scrounged around and came up with a tin of Kipper Snacks. Just what the doctor ordered. Now if I could find some crackers, saltines or Sailor Boy, I'd be all set. But no. Ex-cept for a couple of cans of vegetable soup, the cupboard was bare. Ah, well, Kipper Snacks would do, and then to bed.

The lower bunk was mine. With only about two feet of space between the bunk's sideboard and the bottom of the top bunk, a little technique was required getting in—sort of a flying horizontal approach. And once in, a lot of wriggling and squirming was needed to get yourself into the bag just right. But then I would feel cozy as a papoose. There's a kind of comfort in constriction, so long as it's more like a hug than a stranglehold. You can suspend your inner effort to maintain yourself because the outer bonds are snug and firm. I imagined a sane society would be like that, offering constant support for your human predilections and clear rules to the game, the sort of tribal context our "primitive" forebears enjoyed.

The last thing I heard was the onshore wind whistling softly across the exhaust pipe. I was glad the boat wasn't down in the water, tied off the dock. Getting a good night's sleep had become my secret obsession.

I didn't hear him climb on board, but I woke with a start when the cabin door opened and he came heavily down the three steps. I raised up on an elbow, twisting around to see who it was. I thought it might be Pope, drunk and wanting to talk. Whoever it was, I resented the intrusion.

The man's outline was large, and he stood there a moment, swaying slightly.

"Hey. You got a cigarette?" The voice was guttural and the accent unmistakably native.

"Yeah. Who's that?"

"You know me, Mike. You son of a bitch!"

He lurched over and dropped down on the seat across from me. I could barely see him, but I was sure I didn't know him.

"Willie. Willie Mulkeit. You know me, you son of a bitch!"

Oh, no. I became fully awake. My blood pressure must have shot up ten points. Flight or fight. Willie Mulkeit was a name I knew. He was one of the two or three most notorious of Dillingham's tigers—tiger being the title earned by certain men

known to be both exceptionally tough and exceptionally ber-
serk. To be regarded as exceptional in these matters down in
Bristol Bay was a mark of distinction not to be taken lightly.
Being a tiger in Bristol Bay was not the same as being the biggest
bully on the block or the baddest jock at school. Tiger meant
assault and battery and, now and then, homicide.

I assumed an alert and studied calm.

"I think there's a couple of butts left in the pack there in
my jacket," I offered, pointing to where it hung on a hook near
his head.

He looked at me for a minute, heavy-eyed, slack-mouthed
from the booze, which I could smell on his breath from across
the cabin. His head was bobbing like a cobra's. No telling what
he was seeing or thinking. He was in his own movie. Best be
prepared for whatever.

"There, right by your head," I said quietly. "I think there's
a couple left."

I hoped there were a couple left. He twisted around and
reached up, and after a tense moment or two pulled out the
flattened pack of Marlboros. He stared at the package, then
across at me.

"You got no Luckies?"

"Nope," I replied in a light, airy way. "That's it. Just those
Marlboros."

"You smoke Luckies, you son of a bitch, Mike. Where's the
fucking Luckies?"

"Hey, no. I don't have any Luckies. I don't smoke them. And
I'm not Mike, Willie. I'm Bob. Bob Durr."

"Who?"

"Bob Durr. Gene Pope's partner."

I hoped I wasn't invoking a wrong name, that one of Pope's
conquests hadn't been Willie's favorite little sister.

"The Professor," I explained. I chuckled a little, wanting to
keep it light and friendly. "Most of the guys call me the Professor."

"The Perfessa?"

He lit the cigarette, and I got a flash of his face: broad cheek-bones, a mashed nose, powerful jaws. In the brief glow of the match, his bony features, bands of light and darkness, might as well have been those of an actual tiger crouched across from me.

"You're Mike Schultz, you son of a bitch. I know you. I ought to punch your fucking lights out. Cocksucker!"

My muscles went hard; I didn't have to tell them to. But if he started for me, I would be helpless. The bunk didn't provide a situation wherein I could move quickly, and I was zipped up in my sleeping bag like a mummy anyway.

"No. Hey, Willie, you got me mixed up with someone else," I started, meanwhile trying to inch the zipper down. "I don't even *know* Mike Schultz. My name's Bob. Bob Durr. The Professor." I tried a little laugh, hoping it wouldn't sound as hollow to him as it did to me.

There was no honor involved in this, only something to be avoided if possible. He sat there smoking. The end of the cigarette glowed and went dark, his bony, stupefied face emerging and fading.

"You got something to eat?"

Shit! Now I knew I was in a tight spot. The Eskimo shared (*The more you have, the more you have to share*) and the white man didn't (*I got mine: Fuck you*). The request for food was a kind of test: Which sort of man was I? He would think I was lying. Goddamn white man! What's in a name? A white man by any other name than Schultz would still be a goddamn white man son of a bitch.

"Oh, wow," I said, in earnest. "You know, I was looking for something myself before, and damned if the larder ain't bare. Just a couple of cans of soup left."

My voice sounded remarkably calm and casual, considering how much adrenaline was pumping through me. The zipper was down to my knees.

"You got no crackers?"

Most boats at least had some Sailor Boy crackers on board.

"No! You know, that's just what I was after before, and I couldn't lay my hands on one." My voice expressed amazement: Can you believe it? No crackers! "But you're welcome to the soup."

I leaned across, pointing to the bin next to the sink, at the same time working the bag down off my feet. I wanted at least a fighting chance. The idea of being pulverized in my bunk was especially repugnant. And I felt myself starting to get aggravated. The time could come when I'd rage, "Tiger or no tiger, I've had enough."

Then I had an inspiration. He probably could see me even less clearly than I could see him, because I was in the shadow of the overhead bunk. If I could reach the light maybe he could see me well enough despite the smog in his head to accept the fact that I wasn't the guy he had it in for. It wasn't likely he would be wanting to muck out just *any* goddamn white man. On the pretext of lighting his way to the food bin, I managed to twist up half out of the bunk and pull the light cord.

"Go ahead, see for yourself, Willie. You're welcome to what you find."

The sudden light dispelled some of the sinister aspect of the scene, even though the bulb was bare. He looked at me blankly, then bent over and reached a hand into the bin, fumbling around, and pulled out one of the cans of Campbell's vegetable soup.

"Not much," I said, "but you're welcome to it." Which he was, and would have been even without the duress.

He tossed the can back and looked at me again.

"Fuck. You ain't Mike."

"Nope," I smiled, quite genuinely. "I told you, I'm Bob Durr, Gene Pope's partner."

"Well, I don't want no soup," he said, looking a little vague. "Bob Duh, huh?" He got up and lurched against the sink. "Well,

Bob Duh, go back to sleep. You ain't even got a biscuit to your name."

He crushed the butt out in the sink, then turned and stuck out his hand. I shook it, and it felt like a knotted manila rope.

"You give me this last cigarette, Bob Duh?" he grinned.

"Sure, Willie. Take it with you." I wanted the idea of departure planted firmly in the damp soil of his mind. "I won't be smoking anymore tonight. Going right back to sleep."

With that he staggered up the steps, and I reached up and switched off the light.

When I heard him above, I got out of the bunk. He might change his mind, or he might think he had just climbed on board. But I heard him go down the ladder, and I listened as his footsteps faded away into the dawn's early light. Then I went above and pulled the ladder up and laid it on the deck.

I got back into the bunk and lay there. I understood the way he was. I was sorry about it. I was sorry he couldn't see I wasn't the same kind as those goddamn white men who had fucked him over, him and his people. Sometimes I felt like a renegade to my race. Willie and so many others like him were lost and staggering around in the void between two antipathetical cultures. The Eskimo, the Indians of both continents, all the original people, the old consciousness, the human beings, everywhere lied to, stolen from, enslaved, and murdered, their age-old ways of life—their very minds and souls—ripped off by the clean-machine power lust and greed of the humanoid whites, creatures alienated from their own nature, assassins of the very earth that bore them.

I couldn't doze off again, and then the cannery crews started up, the machines went on, and that was the end of *that* good night's sleep.

❋

At first Dillingham to me meant the cannery dock complex overlooking the bay. The town itself was inconsequential, a background. In a sense my impression was correct, for the cannery was the town's main reason for being. Dillingham was there because of the salmon. During the sixties there were two canning companies in Dillingham, the New England Fish Company (NEFCO) and Pacific Alaska Fisheries (PAF). At that time they had combined their operations and facilities in Dillingham, so that although some fishermen sold to NEFCO and some to PAF, in terms of the overall operation it was one big company with two sets of books.

The cannery buildings were all gray corrugated sheet metal—the canning facility, the machine shop, the carpenter's shack, the net loft, the mess hall, everything. Everything was covered with the same gray corrugated sheet metal, very hard-nosed, very businesslike. Everything except the boss's house. He and his wife lived in a white frame house back away from the dock area. It was set back from the dirt road as well, and was further removed from the daily grind by a picket fence. Dillingham might be a rough frontier town, but it was still America: on the one hand, the workers and the workplace, where the money is made, and on the other the boss's big white house, where most of the money goes. Nevertheless the boss's house also had a roof of corrugated gray sheet metal. The cannery wasn't doing nearly as well as Chrysler Motors.

The dock area turned into Dillingham as you walked away from it, part of the way across some planks where it got muddy. There were no paved streets or sidewalks. Besides the post office on the ground floor of the only modern-looking apartment complex in town, downtown was mainly the B&C Commercial Company, a large frame building that looked as if it belonged in a New England seacoast town. It carried expensive groceries and various nautical gear such as boots and heavy-duty black Norwegian slickers. A little off from the B&C was the Sea Inn Bar. For the fishermen, this was the real heart of town.

The main gravel road came down a gentle hill toward the cannery, then turned west and ran out of town, past the small-boat harbor and, a mile or so farther, past the Willow Tree Inn and then the little airport, to terminate at the Native Hospital about five miles south on a bluff overlooking the bay. Approximately halfway between town and the small-boat harbor, Tent City sprouted each year during the fishing season—a couple of dozen tents of every vintage and size set up in a weedy field beside the road. Its population was composed almost exclusively of Eskimo from the villages who had come to fish out of Dillingham. It was time to fish, and so they set up their tents as they had always done. For the younger ones, especially the teenagers, the summer fishing season was like an extended holiday in the big city. Gene Pope was well known among the Eskimo of Bristol Bay. Pilots and captains of fish boats were like movie stars to the young ladies, and Pope was a regular celebrity visitor to Tent City.

Dillingham was altogether void of country clubs or cultural amenities. But, for compensation, it had character. It was real. It was a hard-core fishing town that had no idea at all that anyone might expect it to look like a picturesque village on a calendar or movie set. So for me Dillingham had the glamour of authenticity, of being in good faith an Alaskan fishing port and cannery town. I walked down the alternately dusty or muddy roads with people who lived lives tied to the elements, on intimate terms with wind, water, and weather, many of them Eskimo, Aleuts, or Athabaskan Indians, people whose forebears and culture glowed like a beacon in my mind, guiding me into the deep channels of our human nature. In search of my own humanity amid the storm of modern insanities, I looked to the first peoples, the "primitives," to keep me on course. The individual native today, I saw with dismay, had been largely disinherited of his birthright, but his culture, his head space, what once he was and to some extent continued to be, was a master light to my understanding, and I held these men and women among whom I moved in 1964 in respect.

So while Dillingham wouldn't be home for me, it had a meaning for me. And because of that meaning, I liked the town.

❖

"Why, *shit!* They fish anything that'll float over there. Speedboats, canoes, washtubs. It don't matter what. If it'll hold fish, it'll be launched."

That was what Les had said about Bristol Bay back in Kenai when we were remodeling *Port N Storm* and I had expressed some doubts as to the appropriateness of the lady's cartop coiffure.

"*Port N Storm*," Les had assured me, "will probably be the pride of the fleet."

Well, among all the no-nonsense redneck regulation gillnetters and slick new fiberglass sophisticates, *Port N Storm* could be no more than the standout misfit at the annual dance of dollars in the salmon capital of the world. Even the open skiffs outclassed her, for they were to the manner born and spoke the language. *Port N Storm* was an imitation fish boat among the impressively real McCoy, a counterfeit coin whose only purchase was a joke.

Gene Pope must have sized her up as such at first glance. Let it be to his credit that he wasn't put off, didn't care that much about looking right, and for reasons of his own took her, and us, under his wing. But then Pope himself was slightly reprobate, an odd man out, in the eyes of the truly solid citizens of Dillingham (who weren't nearly as solid as the solid citizens of Topeka, Kansas). He was too wild, reckless: shiftless. More into making merry than making money. They mended their nets, fine-tuned their carburetors, and made sure they got a good night's rest before they went fishing. Pope's nets had holes in them a whale could slip through, and he often went fishing roaring drunk at the tail end of the tide after partying all night.

But Pope was never mean, he didn't steal, and he didn't get into fights unless sorely provoked. He was always merry and bright. Despite themselves people smiled when they spoke of Gene Pope. That he was found in company of an oddball like *Port N Storm* was no more than to be expected.

Les and I went about our business regardless of *Port N Storm's* image. After all, this was Alaska, *frontier* Alaska. A man could do what he damn well pleased if there was no law against it, and sometimes especially if there was. Conformity was not counted among the virtues, but the spirit of derring-do was. No one would say you shouldn't do this or that, that it was foolish or too risky. Go for it! If you fell on your face there would be a good laugh in it. And if you made it against all odds, there would be a story worth repeating.

As it happened, Les and I did fairly well with the fishing. We went out with the fleet, caught an average number of fish, and didn't run afoul of anyone. But on shore I sensed a strange resistance to our presence. A subtle thing. Pope marching into Dillingham with us in tow to meet the rest of the guys, and the rest of the guys seeming preoccupied, having things to do, places to go, people to meet. We were on the receiving end of a lot of straight-faced cool looks.

Later, after I learned about "outside fishermen," I figured it out. Pope's gang (eventually identified as D Inn Crowd) were mostly native or partly native. They had been born and raised in Bristol Bay, and their fathers and mothers and grandparents before them, going back, probably, into prehistory. This was their country, and by rights, as they saw it, it was their fish that outsiders like Les and I had come to take. The economics were simple enough. The more boats, the fewer fish per boat. In the bum years, when the salmon pack was small (four out of five years in those days), the native fisherman returning to his village faced a lean winter: Salmon fishing was his main source of income. The outsider, who typically had another job the rest of the year or fished other waters, too, after a poor season might have to postpone buying his wife the new car he had promised her. In the native's view, I didn't need to fish: I had a job, I was a professor. I was in Bristol Bay to take home some extra bucks. To gild my lily. More greedy white-man stuff.

One day early in the season, Les and I climbed the ladder up to the dock after having come in from fishing. We had washed up on board, shaved, changed clothes, and were sporting the white peaked caps many of the fishermen in Bristol Bay wore then. We were heading down to the Sea Inn for a cold beer or two. It was a sunny afternoon, we were feeling pretty good. We had gone out and come back several times and hadn't sunk once. I was feeling especially good. A few swallows do not a summer make, however, and a few times fishing do not a fisherman make; but then, the swallows don't fly in wintertime either: I *was* there, actually fishing in Bristol Bay. The wilderness was getting closer.

Two of Pope's pals, Kenny Brandon and Louie Hereshka, sat on some lumber stacked against a cannery building. Their white shirts accentuated their swarthy complexions. They were mostly native, originally from the Dillingham area but now living in Anchorage. Louie was Kenny's partner, or "boat puller" (the term goes back to the sailboat days, when the hired hand did most of the pulling on the oars). Kenny was owner and captain of the *Wanda B*, a fine fiberglass gillnetter. The Brandons—at the time, three brothers and a sister—were a kind of fishing dynasty in Bristol Bay. Louie was an old friend. Pope had introduced them to us the first night in town, had tried to start up a party, round up the boys, but Kenny and Louie had drifted off in their own directions.

I stopped, said hello, and asked if they had seen Gene around. Les stood off to the side with his hands in his pockets. He had no personal interest in Dillingham or the other fishermen; he had no plans to leave the Kenai.

"Nope, haven't seen him," Kenny replied. His face was blank. He didn't look at me. Louie was gazing out to sea.

Making conversation, I asked, "How'd you guys do today?"

A wrong question. I wasn't one of the guys, and one of the guys wouldn't have asked that question, not straight on like that. It was like asking a Rockefeller how much he was worth.

"Can't complain, y'know," Kenny said dryly. Then turning to Louie, "Guess we better get boogying on down to Billy's."

They got up and, without any further notice of us, walked off. Les and I were strangers. Outside fishermen. That was the only category they had to put us in. What was I to do? Should I have run after them, grasped Kenny's arm, and explained, "Hey! You got me all wrong. I'm not here for the *money*, I want to live like you do. Or did."

Les and I continued on down to the Sea Inn, where, if we had the money, we would be welcome. We sat at the bar among a lot of other fishermen who seemed to know one another. An hour ago we had been out on the bounding main getting knocked around. Now we sat enveloped in soft lights and juke-box music, watching the fish kissing in the aquarium behind the bar as we sipped our beer. Bernice served us. It would be more accurate to say she condescended to accept our dollars in exchange for her beer. A formidable presence, Bernice. She had thick red hair piled high on top of her head and must have been good-looking before she turned into Medusa. She never rested her baleful eyes full upon us, no doubt because stone men don't buy beer. No one joked with her, and certainly no one flirted with her. If the deference these rough men paid her had been legal tender, she would have been rich. She was from the South, and it scrambled my expectations the first time I heard that kind of drawl issue from that intertelluric countenance as we got up to leave.

"Thanks, boys. Y'all come back now, heah?"

❁

The next day we were up early, eager to try our luck again. The morning was bright with promise. Guys were moving around on the boats, freeing lines; engines were starting. We moved out with them and headed down toward Clarks Point at a good clip.

Oddly, a boat up ahead appeared to be drifting with its nets out. What was odd was that we and the drifting boat were way above the upper-limit markers. If Fish and Game spotted them, they would be in real trouble.

"Hey," Les said, leaning forward, "ain't that the *Otter*— Pope's boat?" We were closer now. It was a commercial hull, and maroon: the *Otter*. There was no sign of life on board. The boat drifted lazily on the calm water like a derelict. The tide was ebbing, but it would be quite a while before it carried the *Otter* back down into legal waters.

"We better warn him," Les said in a serious tone. Then he laughed. "The bastard's probably dead-drunk asleep. Ed too."

We hadn't seen Pope for days and had been wondering where he was and what he was up to. It surprised us both that apparently he was out scratch fishing, like a serious fisherman. We knew he didn't care about the money. He had told us money wasn't all that important in the Iliamna country, that he could always get by one way or another. For Pope fishing time was party time; catching fish was a secondary consideration.

We throttled up and bore down on the *Otter*, expecting the sound of our approach to bring Gene or Edwin up on deck. But no one showed, not even as we passed close off their bow. Les turned the wheel and circled back.

"I told you," he said. "They're both dead drunk." Then he let loose his abrupt laugh again. Gene Pope alternately amazed, aggravated, and tickled VanDevere. He cut the engine, and we drifted abreast of the *Otter*.

"Hey, *Pope!*" he yelled.

There was no response.

"Okay," Les said, "both together on the count of three. One, two, *three*." And we both yelled Pope's name at the top of our lungs. We were close enough and loud enough to raise even the dead drunk.

A moment or two later the cabin door on the *Otter* opened. Gene Pope stepped out on deck wearing only a broad smile and white Jockey shorts.

"You're way over the line, Gene!" Les said, some urgency in his voice.

I expected Pope to go straight-faced and look quickly around. Instead, he smiled more broadly, if possible, and flung out his arms. He looked beatific.

"I'm in love!" he bellowed. Then he turned around and went back down into the cabin, where, it flashed upon us, someone other than Edwin awaited him.

Gene Pope was not only over the line, he was across the border and into that other country where most of us would like to linger. There were no laws or fines in that other country, and no consequences. In that country the ecstatic act trammels up the consequences, and there is no tomorrow, or if there is it never comes.

We started up and continued on our way, a little brightened, a little wistful. About Fish and Game, if he wasn't worried, why should we be?

We learned later that Pope had met and immediately fallen in love with a native girl from Dillingham named Teresa. We didn't see much of him the rest of the summer. But one day toward the end of the season he appeared on *Port N Storm* in the small-boat harbor.

"Anybody home?" I heard his voice and looked up from where I was writing a letter to see him stooping at the door, looking in, handsome and sparkling like the young Errol Flynn. "I got someone here I'd like you to meet, Professor."

I had noticed a figure behind him, just the blue-jeaned lower torso visible through the door, but that had been enough to assure me it was a girl. Pope came down, and the girl followed. She was small and pretty in a kind of fifties high school way. She wore her black hair in bangs adorned with a startling red ribbon. Although she was short, she was sturdily built, with an hourglass figure, and she displayed the broad face and high cheekbones of her lineage. She, too, was bright-eyed, and wide-eyed as a three-year-old. Her smile was loose and innocent.

"This here is Teresa," said Pope. He looked down at her with a satisfied smile. He was proud to show her off.

Teresa, like her Dillingham peers, had grown up in a world bombarded by the images and sounds of American pop culture of the fifties. She was an Elvis girl, her inner life exciting and special, always with an exciting and special man. The remnants of the old ways of her people, which bobbed to the surface of her mind occasionally, were just so much flotsam and jetsam. Her skin boat was no longer intact, the walrus hides in shreds. She was adrift on the contemporary currents of circumstance and mayhem, headed for the open seas of nihility.

In the exuberance of his new romance, Pope didn't concern himself with possible ramifications. He was following his nose, not worrying where the trail might lead. Some anthropologists tell us that because of a million-year-old biology, males of our species are not spontaneously monogamous but have to be talked into it by a culture determined to have it that way. If that's true, then Pope was a cultural dropout. He had a tin ear, or a mind that refused to listen. He went with his biology. So there was about him the distinct odor of goat. Obeying laws or moral mandates was not what he had come to Alaska to do. It was after the season of '64 that he took Teresa back with him to Pope-Vannoy Landing, and his wife held his rifle to his stomach, or a little lower, but he talked her out of it.

It wasn't my place or inclination to judge my friend. What did I know about the inner workings of his marriage with Matrona? No one outside a marriage can know, and therefore no one outside a marriage can judge. Moreover, Gene Pope had no intention of conducting himself according to the complex of cultural laws and ethical imperatives operative in the civilized world. All those he had fled as a youth. He was in this sense an outlaw. In city and suburb the constraints of rules and regulations crowd the atmosphere almost palpably. But in the wilderness they fall away to silence, and the air is clear and open to natural predilections. The woods impose no demands and make no judgments.

At the close of that first fishing season, Les and I parted company. He took his share of the proceeds and his nets back to the Kenai, having decided that after all he preferred to fish Cook Inlet, home territory that he knew and where he was known. Bristol Bay's reception had been rather cool and its operation a bit too high-powered, a bit too commercial. He preferred Cook Inlet's homemade style. He had wanted to see what it was like in Bristol Bay, and he had, and that was enough. He was satisfied to go home with a few bucks in his pocket and a few stories in his head. For my part, although I hadn't seen all that much of Pope after we arrived in Dillingham, I knew there was something special between him and me, a connection had been made, a friendship started.

I had made arrangements with Dr. Bud Bergner, then in charge of the Fisheries Research Institute of the University of Washington, to be winter man at their station on Lake Nerka, the second of the beautiful Woods River chain of lakes north of Dillingham. I would keep weather records and data on the fish caught through the ice, preserving entrails and scales, in exchange for living in their cabin. My family would join me there in September. I had won a Guggenheim Fellowship to write a book and was thus free of my responsibilities at Syracuse University. The focus of the present book, however, is on my effort to prove up as a fisherman as the necessary first step to moving me and my family into the woods for good (or for better or worse), so I won't digress here about the winter on Lake Nerka other than to say it confirmed my idea that wilderness life suited family life. The kids loved it, and Carol had no problem adjusting to the simplicity, rigors, and isolation of that life. But as I said, all that is for another book, when I tell the full story of the family's venture.

❀

The immediate plan was for Carol and the three younger kids to return to our New York home in the spring and for me and my eldest son Steve to stay on in Alaska to fish with Pope on the *Otter* in the season of '65.

## 4

## OUR FIRST BIG RUN, '65

The year 1965 was a big one in Bristol Bay. The salmon runs peaked every fifth year in those days, and for 1965 the run was expected to be enormous. Fish and Game would easily get their escapement quota, with millions of fish left for the fishermen and processors. It was generally calculated that the average boat would net about twenty grand of 1960s dollars in about two to three weeks of intense harvesting. At the height of such a run the canneries would be forced to put an upper limit on the number of fish each boat could deliver during a single period, because they couldn't handle any more. In 1965 the limit was two thousand fish per boat per period. If the fish were all caught on one drift, as was often the case, that would be a lot of weight to pull in over the roller, two thousand sockeyes averaging around five pounds each, and a lot of weight to ask a boat to carry, especially in rough water. For some of the older narrow-beamed boats it was more than they should attempt. But in the frenzy of that kind of fishing, with everyone's nets smoking, it was hard to stay cool enough to calculate your own safe limits, and sometimes the fish were so thick in the water they could plug your nets before you realized it was happening or before you could get your gear out of the water. In some cases the nets sank to the bottom with the load. Many thousands of fish and a lot of gear were lost that way. And it was at such times that boats and fishermen were lost, too.

The major portion of the Bristol Bay run that year was forecast for the Naknek-Kvichak watershed, but it was always a gamble whether the Nushagak or the Naknek-Kvichak would prove to be the best bet. A fisherman could transfer either way, but if his choice proved wrong, he lost a lot of precious time. The height of the run could pass through in a matter of days. The trip from Nushagak Bay to Naknek or vice versa took about ten hours, and a transferred boat once there had to wait another period before it was permitted to transfer back if it turned out the captain had bet on the wrong watershed. Then, of course, another day would be lost in the return trip.

> *The fishing's hot at Naknek, I heard it today*
> *Gas her up and head her out of Nushagak Bay*
> *You meet a bunch of boats a-coming back the other way*
> *They say the nets are all smoking up in Nushagak Bay*
>
> *Hard times on the water, down in Bristol Bay*

Pope had written me a few times during the winter. He said he had refurbished the old *Otter*, enlarged the pilothouse, and built extra bunks in the rearranged cabin. The boat would now sleep four. A gillnetter that slept four was unprecedented, and the four Gene Pope envisioned on board were even more so: Teresa, for instance. Pope had determined he couldn't possibly let Teresa languish ashore while he was away at sea, so he planned to bring her along. We would be a jolly crew, Pope and I philosophizing or singing sea chanteys, with Steve joining in, and Teresa brimming with pride and joy as she fixed the victuals. This scenario constituted a new concept in commercial salmon fishing: no more strictly down to business because the dollar is king, but instead a communism of work as play in a world where the dollar has no dominion. In the cosmic courtroom, however,

the Antagonist, still in office, must have gotten word of these
Edenic plans and petitioned the Judge to let him throw something—a monkey wrench or a woman, say—into the works if
for no other reason than to remind those vagrants down there
that they were, being human, born to trials and tribulations, not
to fun and games.

❀

We were about an hour past Clarks Point on our maiden voyage
to Naknek on the born-again *Otter*, already late on the tide
because we had had to wait for Teresa, and for the same reason
at least a day or two late to be starting across, since the salmon
had already begun to arrive in considerable numbers over there,
when Pope announced regretfully that we would have to turn
back, yes, even bucking the tide, because Teresa had developed
a real bad stomachache. He wore his serious and sincere look,
and I could see he felt assured of my immediate acquiescence
and concern. But what Teresa was suffering from was menstrual
cramps, and I undertook to convince Pope that, with all due
sympathy and commiseration for the female condition, a run to
the doctor really wasn't necessary. He didn't want to turn back
either, so my greater experience in these matters prevailed; and
since I was the one who had objected to turning back in the
first place, Pope didn't even lose much solicitous ground with
Teresa.

The upshot of it was that I got to steer. Pope was sure that
all greenhorns loved to be at the wheel just as much as he hated
to be. So he remained below comforting Teresa while I took us
across to the Naknek side. I did ask for some directions, though.
The one spacey trip over from Naknek the year before did not,
I felt, qualify me as a pilot. And I had no intention of retracing
Pope's route through Dead Man's Sands.

"Don't worry," he assured me. "You can't get us into any

trouble I can't get us out of. Just stay far enough offshore around Etolin Point and look for Johnson Hill on your right after you make the turn. Then you'll know you're on course!"

He flashed his death's-head smile and without further ado or advice disappeared below. My pride refused to let my better judgment inquire any further. I was at the wheel, the smooth wooden spokes in hand, captain in command of the vessel, and that was that. The devil take the hindmost.

Down the rest of the bay the going was easy, the water laid back, innocent, seemingly incapable of being roused. But as we were somewhere abreast of Etolin Point (a misnomer inasmuch as the flat sweep of land so named formed a wide arc, not a point) the wind picked up and so did the waves. They picked us up and dropped us down with increasing gusto as we moved out of the bay into the whole sweep of ocean blowing in from Japan. Earlier that spring when I felled a tree for firewood, the butt of it took an unexpected bounce and cracked one of my ribs. Now, with the *Otter* pounding so hard, it began complaining: It didn't like all the vigorous muscular activity it was being subjected to. Just staying on my feet, however, required vigorous muscular activity. I ignored my rib, though it never stopped protesting. An hour before, Steve had turned pale, and after he had leaned over the side a couple of times I suggested he go below, take my lower bunk, which would roll less, and hope that he would feel better after a while. That left me alone with the wheel and the ocean of my thoughts.

How round was Etolin Point? How many miles to round it? How far offshore was far enough? How sharp or dull a left turn must I be making in order to round Etolin Point without running into the shoals or hitting Dead Man's Sands or, on the other hand, without heading out to open ocean? If I spotted Johnson Hill, the sole landmark in the whole vast area, I would know I had made the left turn right, so to speak. But if I didn't spot Johnson Hill I would be literally very much at sea. And *when* should I expect to spot Johnson Hill, given the variables of wind, wave, tide, knots per hour, and the vagaries of my route? That is, how long should I hang tough before I panicked and casually called for Pope to come up and have a look around?

I was steering by the sun, with a little help from the compass. But the sun was disappearing among the roiling clouds more and more frequently and for longer and longer periods, and the compass was spinning like a slow-motion top as I tacked, trying to keep the big waves off the starboard or port bow because the wind coming in off the ocean was pushing the seas at us broadside to the way we had to go. I didn't want to broach those waves.

Hour after hour went by with all of life reduced to gauging the character of the next wave and trying to keep track of the fugitive sun. That's all there was to life—just the waves and the sun. I became so tired and my side hurt so insistently that somewhere around the sixth or seventh hour the tension broke like a fever and I passed into that peculiar kind of careless high I had first experienced crossing Dead Man's Sands with Les the year before. I started singing:

> Yo ho ho and a bottle of rum
> Sixteen men on a dead man's chest

"Big man!" I said out loud. "Sixteen men on his chest! So that's how he died." And I laughed out loud, too.

The waves were getting bigger all the while, sporting dashing breakers along their ridges. And they had individuality. Some were a lot bigger than the general population, some were longer, some shorter, and some came on as a single broad band, while others broke into separate war parties. So long as I managed to meet them slightly off either side of the bow, compromising between a pitch and a roll, we rode them well enough. But now and then, when I was moving into a tack, a couple would hit us dead on, and it was as though we had gone right down into the sea and been engulfed. No deck, no sky, only rushing water.

But each time miraculously the windshield would drain, and I could see our bow knifing up out of the foam into the sky. Or a mean one would catch us almost broadside, and the *Otter* would roll horribly onto her side. Anything in the enlarged pilothouse, which doubled as a pantry, that wasn't nailed down took off on its own and whizzed across to the opposite side. At times things like forks and spoons, boxes of tea or crackers, and an occasional mug or plate were flying around as though by demonic command. I marveled that my shipmates remained below, maybe even sleeping peacefully, finding the minimized motion of the hold soothing.

It seemed to me I should have spotted Johnson Hill some time ago, but there weren't even any obscure landmarks to indicate my position. The broad apron of shoal water became land quite imperceptibly. I knew that land lay off my port side somewhere, but I couldn't make out any sign of it. I recalled that when VanDevere and I were studying maps and charts of the region the year before, on one of them Les noticed a circled dot near Etolin Point with the word TREE printed next to it. He let out a whoop: Was that piece of territory so flat and undistinguished that a lone tree merited notation? One tree—by now probably part of someone's woodpile or gone up in smoke. No use looking for landmarks in that direction. I had followed the sun's intermittent appearances as it arced slowly across the sky behind the clouds, and according to my best calculations I had to be generally on course—maybe a little too close to the west side, in which case I had to watch out for Dead Man's Sands. I checked the Fathometer again (I had bought one for the *Otter*). The amber electronic digits assured me we were still in plenty of water. But, then again, we could have been heading too far east, too far out to sea, which would explain why Johnson Hill hadn't appeared yet: We had missed the entrance to the bay and were on our way to Japan.

There was a chart in a canvas sling on the bulkhead below. If I could check it I would be surer of my bearings in relation to the compass reading. I didn't want to yell for anyone. Having come this far into the trip on my own, I wanted to go the rest of the way on my own. I left the wheel, leaped across and down a step, and grabbed the chart, then hopped back up. The wheel was spinning as though under invisible and probably insidious hands. I stopped it and looked quickly around. Everything was awry, turned around. The waves were coming from the *port* side, and the glimmer of sun had flipped to the opposite rim of the sky. I was turned around in more ways than one. My mind spun in centrifugal confusions for a few bad moments. Which way were we pointed now? If the waves were coming from the port side and the glint of sun was now behind me, we must have done a 180. I swung the *Otter* about—back on course, I hoped.

Unrolled, the chart was large and unruly. I was trying to watch the waves, steer, and at the same time take a peek at the chart, but it kept rolling itself back up. Finally I held the wheel with my stomach and chest (cracked rib screaming again) and spread the chart out with both hands. According to my interpretation of what I saw there (which left plenty of room for error to roam around in), I had been heading more or less right all along. The boat lurched from a wave. I grabbed the wheel and let the chart snap back to its preferred cylindrical form. Then, just to the right of the metallic sheen of the sun as a big wave lifted us aloft, I saw in the distance a dim and inconspicuous promontory directly off the starboard bow, right where it was supposed to be. Brave Balboa topping the rise to behold the mighty Pacific Ocean stretching away before his eyes could not have been more elated than I to detect the pale granular shape of Johnson Hill on the horizon. That Balboa's discovery made history, whereas mine wouldn't even make the news, was of no personal moment. I was very glad to see Johnson Hill. I started singing again, in the biggest voice I had left.

*In Dillingham there dwells a maid*
*She is the mistress of her trade*

*And I'll go no more a-roving with you, fair maid—*
*A-roving, a-roving, it's roving's been my ruin*
*And I'll go no more a-roving with you, fair maid*

That brought Pope up on deck. I didn't say anything, didn't even turn my head, just gazed straight ahead. He looked at me, then glanced around. In my peripheral vision I saw him focus on Johnson Hill. A bright smile broke over his face.

"Well, captain," he said, beaming at me like a general about to award a medal, "looks like you earned your merit badge. All *right!*"

With that, he clapped me on the back, provoking an especially sharp protest from my rib, which wasn't interested in congratulations.

❁

The Naknek River was just as frenetic as it had been the year before when I first saw it, even more so—fish boats running about in all directions, hundreds at anchor or tied off the docks, the big scows looking like mother hens surrounded by energetic chicks. We had arrived in between periods, but you could see the place was vibrating with excitement. The run was coming on full bore, every bit as big as predicted. Some boats were delivering more than two thousand fish already; a limit had not yet been imposed, but it was expected soon.

After we tied up, Gene and Teresa (she was feeling much better after her long rest) took off uptown—a dirt road with scattered frame buildings, a bar, and a couple of musty stores among the saw grass. Teresa had relatives in Naknek, and she and Gene would probably spend the night ashore. That was okay with me and Steve, who was also feeling better now but who had been sick and miserable the whole trip. We were interested in only one thing: sleep. If my rib would forgive and forget I would do my part, being perfectly willing to lie still in my bunk, relinquished to sweet oblivion. You never know what is enough until you know what is too much, said Blake. I knew I had had enough of sailing for that day.

The following morning, with Gene and Teresa back on board, we ran over to the west side, somewhere between Half Moon Bay and the Banana Trees, where the hottest action was reported. The designation Half Moon Bay is clear enough, obviously describing the shape of the land-water configuration it denotes. But Banana Trees, in Alaska, was a bit of a puzzle at first, especially in this part of Alaska, where the existence of *any* tree gets noted on a chart. But then I came to understand the fisherman's propensity to speak in metaphor and code. When you pull in a net densely loaded with salmon, the clustered fish coming over the roller could be said to resemble bunches of bananas. At least, some time ago it struck an imaginative fisherman that way: "Why, shit, man, they were so thick they looked like bunches of bananas!" The image caught on. So when some time afterward a guy hit into the fish in a big way and, looking around for a landmark on shore to mark the hot spot, he saw a clump of big bushes, he naturally referred to the spot as the Banana Trees. And that name caught on, too, as bits of poetry often do, even among the macho crowd.

The day was sunny and the seas moderate. As we cruised around looking for a nice open spot among all the boats, we saw hits, geysers of spray and quivering corks, up and down all the nets we passed. We were in the right place at the right time. The water was shivering and sparkling with salmon, and the nets were alive with their captured power.

Pope was at the wheel, sleeves rolled up, looking around with a satisfied grin on his face, and nodding. "Yes sir," he said, "we're right on time, Professor. All aboard the gravy train!"

In high spirits, we found a slot a bit away from the central congestion of boats, hoping we were still where the fish were traveling, and started laying out the net. Fish like torpedoes exploding hit the net as soon as it touched the water, six, eight at a time, without letup. Under a haze and sparkle of spray the corkline quivered and danced, in places bowed a fathom or more out of line by slugs of fish powerfully trying to push through. There had been nothing like this the year before with Les. I stood by the wheel, my eyes on Steve standing with Pope in the stern watching the fish hit. Pope was taller and huskier, Steve trim and athletic, just starting to fill out, his blond hair tossing in the wind, his face clean-cut and ruddy now from the weather. He was—all of us are—made for this kind of life, a physical life in the open air molding the human form and spirit to the contours of the natural world. His blue eyes were wide open, and I could see the excitement in his body as he watched. This was his first drift, his first experience fishing for salmon in Bristol Bay, and it didn't get any better. I was glad he was there to see this prodigality of nature's bounty, nature in full flood, abundance overflowing. It was a spectacular sight and would live in his memory, and one day, when he would hear of skeleton stocks and failing fisheries, he would know that man's stupidity and greed, not nature's providence, was to blame, for he had witnessed the generosity of its giving at firsthand. The enormous numbers of carrier pigeons darkening the sky, the great herds of buffalo and caribou covering plain and tundra, the vast migrations of herds in Africa—these and so much more of the wildlife of the planet had been swept into oblivion by the predations of progress and were gone forever. But in Alaska's Bristol Bay in 1965 the sea was aflame with millions upon millions of sockeye salmon burning to reach their natal streams and, like the phoenix, die into new life. The nets were *smoking*.

This was an occasion when our unprecedented four-person crew was none too many. We had heavy loads of bananas to pull on board. After only a few minutes Pope reckoned we had better haul in the nets before they overloaded and sank. The hydraulic roller quit at once (it hadn't signed on for that kind of heavy duty). All four of us pulled, the two extra backs partly making up for the lost power of the roller. Even so, we had to pull with all our might, Pope and I on either side in the stern and Teresa and Steve behind us in the picking bins.

We all wore hip boots. Steve and I were in our rain gear as well. Pope was in shirtsleeves, with a rubber apron covering him in front. Teresa wore his rain jacket, which came down below her knees. When you pull in a loaded net you get spattered with water, fish slime, and blood.

By the time the first shackle was in, the fish were packed tight about my legs and I couldn't move. I continued hauling on the lead line as I struggled to free my legs. The muscles of my forearms cramped with pain until I couldn't grip the line, but my fingers curled into rigid hooks and I pulled with my body weight instead of just with my arms. We needed to get the fish in as soon as possible, before the nets got plugged and we lost them—or before we had too many fish for the old *Otter,* too much weight in the stern, too little freeboard left. All it would take then would be one or two waves hurdling the gunwale and the endless ranks of the rest would overrun us like barbarian hordes flooding into a town whose walls had failed.

We were in shallow water off the beach. As we pulled the boat under the net (which is what is really happening when you "pull the net in"), we were inching away from shore, which was good, because the wind was wanting to push us onto the beach, where both waves and boats broke.

All but two-thirds of the last shackle was in. Pope had set Teresa to picking the easy fish as fast as she could, tossing them up forward into the fish hold, to get weight out of the stern. She had tired completely at the pulling. Pope handled the lead line alone, a strong man with experienced muscles, while Steve and I pulled on the corkline.

We were down to the last few fathoms of net when we bumped bottom. The waves had been building up a bit with the strengthening wind. We bumped again, harder. Steve threw me a look. The *Otter* was ass heavy; we could be in trouble. Pope, as usual, knew just what to do. He handed me the lead line and told us to keep on pulling, then scrambled up forward, started the engine, and threw it into reverse. That cut us some slack and made it a little easier to haul the clumps of fish over the roller. We needed to get the rest of the net in before we did much more bottom knocking (if you keep knocking on Davy Jones's locker, he will let you in). We hit lightly again, then harder, and Pope goosed the engine a little. Too much! The net went slack. Steve and I pulled as fast as we could with a surge of adrenaline, but some webbing caught the prop and stopped it dead.

"Shit!" Pope roared.

Teresa straightened and looked quickly up at him. She had lived long enough among fishermen to understand that our situation was not good. "What do we do now, Gene?" she asked, appearing a little frightened. I was wondering the same thing. We were sitting low in the stern, bouncing off the bottom, the waves were building up, pushing us toward the breakers along the beach, and we had just lost power. All three of us turned toward Pope: *What do we do now, Gene?*

"Shit and go blind! Shit and go blind!" he bellowed. "What else can we do?" Then, seeing the expressions on our faces, he burst into a laugh that doubled him over. I was amazed to see him joking at a time like that, and not just a grim battlefield kind of joke but, in his one-of-a-kind mind, a belly-laugh joke, real laughter.

"Fuck you, Gene," Teresa shot back, miffed, forgetting her fright. She pulled off the slicker, threw it down, and climbed up forward, pushing past him and into the pilothouse. We bumped bottom again, a jolt that ran through the boat and up my legs and into my mind, stirring things up.

Pope ripped off his apron and threw it down with the same gesture Teresa had used. For a moment I thought, incredulously, that they were just going to settle down to a good fight while we either swamped or cracked open. Fiddling while Rome burned.

"Women!" he said, straight-faced, shooting a glance at me. Then he picked up a coil of line and tied an end around his waist. "Either of you guys got a good sharp knife?"

I did, but I hesitated. I had no idea what he was up to. A sharp knife? A line tied around his middle? Pope was not predictable. Steve stood stock-still with his hands clamped on the corkline. He looked at Pope and then at me.

Pope smiled. "I'm gonna play frogman, Professor," he explained. "I'll try to cut the webbing out of the wheel." He was all business now, focused on the job at hand. I got the knife out of my pocket. He worked his way back to us, then cinched the free end of the line to the stern cleat. "Maybe I can get to it without going all the way in. I'll go headfirst. You guys get ahold of my legs and pull me back after a reasonable amount of time, or if I start kicking hard." He regarded our wide eyes with some amusement. "The rope's just in case I slip through your hands."

Without waiting for our commentary, he slipped out of his boots and doffed his shirt. I was thinking of that frigid water. He thrust his hand out toward me, wearing his tight-lipped smile. Was he about to shake hands good-bye?

"The knife, Professor," he said.

The knife! I handed it to him, and he opened the lockout blade and tested the edge with a thumb. "Sharper than the rest of us," he said. And then, with the knife between his teeth, he started over the side, headfirst. Steve and I each grabbed a leg. He went in past his knees, with Steve and me leaning way over, hanging on to his ankles. Jesus! I was thinking, what if we bounce hard and he gets his head knocked on the bottom or maybe an arm smashed under the skeg?

His body was wriggling and his legs too, probably only from his efforts and the motion of the waves, but I was wanting to pull him back when Steve said, "Here's Freeman." I glanced back in the direction he was looking just as Freeman Roberts, a young native we had met earlier, was climbing on board out of his skiff. I had heard an engine close by but had been too preoccupied with Gene to pay it any mind. Freeman tied his skiff alongside, then looked at us.

"What's that?" he asked. "The water cure? Pope hungover? Or is this a mutiny?"

Just then Gene kicked his legs, and we hauled him back into the boat, a segment of net dripping from his hand. He saw Freeman standing there in his sou'wester hat with the brim turned up in front, a bemused expression on his face. This was a challenge Pope met easily, gleefully.

"Hey, Freeman, you're just in time," he said. "Surf's up, and the water's wet." He stood with his hands on his hips, grinning, his black curls plastered to his head and dripping.

We bounced off the bottom again.

Over all the years I knew Gene Pope, I never saw him get serious about a serious situation. On the contrary, the hairier things got, the more exuberant he got. It sometimes seemed to me that if circumstances didn't spontaneously generate a crisis or two, he would manufacture one. The ordinary course of events, even in Alaska, just couldn't provide the challenge— the Adventure!—on which he thrived. Being safe was beneath notice.

Without stopping to dry off, still in his dripping pants and socks, he scrambled up to the pilothouse and started the engine. "I think I got enough of it so we have some power," he said. With the wheel hard to port, this time he threw it into forward, hoping to turn away from the beach. We were moving, slowly, but with a *clunk-clunk* you could feel. Some corks and fish were still wrapped around the propeller shaft. And we were still bouncing off the bottom. If we could ease back into deeper water, then maybe we could free the prop the rest of the way and retrieve the last fathom or so of net still in the water (and no doubt plugged).

Steve and I started picking fish, throwing them up forward, working fast. Freeman, an experienced hand, pitched in, too. The thought crossed my mind that if the worst should come to the worst and we swamped, at least we wouldn't have to swim for it: Freeman's skiff could hold us all.

Teresa had come back out on deck when Pope went over the side. Now she was trying to dry him off with a sweater. "Gene," she admonished with a big smile, her bunched cheeks like baked apples, "I can't dry all of you with those pants on." She had a hoarse voice, even when she laughed, which she did now as she reached for his belt buckle.

"Not now, woman!" He pretended to push her away, while still minding what he was doing, but then she had his pants and shorts down and was drying him. "Have you no shame!" he protested. "In front of my friends!" They were both laughing as we bumped slowly ahead, barely gaining on the wind and tide, in danger, as a matter of fact, of swamping.

"That boat's gonna *swamp!*"

Pope's arm shot out. He was pointing off the starboard side. In the instant before I turned to look, the sight of his stance, bent forward from the waist with his arm stretched straight out, naked with his pants around his ankles, released a quick ripple of laughter in my otherwise mirthless mind. But then I saw the boat, an old double-ender, originally one of the sailboat fleet, now converted to power. It was under way, moving ahead very slowly. Its bow was tilted so far up in the air I wondered how the man at the wheel could see where he was going. But that wasn't their main problem. To the same degree that the bow was high, the stern was low. It looked as if they had run out of freeboard back there. One wave crashing over would invite the rest, and they would all accept.

Two figures were bent over in the stern picking fish. Either they didn't see any reason to hurry or they were new to the job and therefore slow. In either case it was clear to me at first glance, as it had been to Pope, that they were about to swamp. The two fish pickers, even if they had been fast, could never get enough pounds up forward before the first outsize wave broke through the thin line of their defense.

We assumed the boat was coming over to us for help. Pope pulled his pants up and slipped into his shirt. We all stood ready to do what we could. The double-ender, however, continued on its way, passing slowly across our bow. The two figures in the stern didn't even look up but remained bent over, picking fish as though, aptly enough, their lives depended on it.

They went right on by. We stood watching them. It seemed almost surreal—this episode in the real world—and absurd, contrary to every reasonable expectation. I think we were all about to burst out laughing, forgetting our own problems for the moment, when, as we watched, the boat took the inevitable wave over the stern and was filling very quickly with water. Now it turned toward us, ponderously. It came close by, bobbing in slow, heavy motion, but the water reached the engine before they were alongside, and it was adrift.

The two men in the stern had climbed up to the bow. By the time we reached their side, the yellow water had filled the hull like a bathtub. The third man on board stood up to his crotch in the water and debris as he handed the marine radio he had rescued up to one of his partners. We dropped our bilge pump into their hold and starting pumping. But we might just as well have dropped it into the ocean. More water was coming in, and faster, than we could possibly pump out.

Nevertheless, crippled as we were ourselves, we would try to save the boat and the fish. Pope was in his element. We tied up to her and helped the three young guys climb onto the *Otter*. They were soaked, of course, dripping water, shivering violently, and they seemed vague or dazed. Teresa hustled them into the cabin, and Steve went along to do what he could. He later told me the one fellow, a lad in his teens, like himself, just sat there shivering in his soaked clothes with his back against a bunk staring blankly, not speaking at all, perhaps in shock, pale looking. Teresa lit the stove, and Steve helped him out of his wet clothes and bundled him into the bunk, and he gradually came around. The other two just dried off a little, wrapped up in blankets, and when it was ready drank hot coffee. They too had been shaking uncontrollably. The waters of Bristol Bay are still frigid in early July. Pope could take it because he was part seal.

We would try to get the double-ender, which was still afloat, over to the nearest scow, whose boom and tackle, winches, and giant bilge pumps could be used to bail her out. But with the swamped boat alongside we could make no headway with the little power we had. We undid the lines, let her drop back slowly, and then tied her off our stern cleat. Pope opened the throttle, but it didn't seem we were actually moving ahead. The clunking around our propeller grew louder and faster. The waves had gotten bigger. We started hitting bottom again. The heavy line between the two boats jerked taut, went slack, and the bow of the double-ender punched a hole in our stern just above the waterline. Freeman jumped over to let out more line, but the dead weight of the swamped boat had cinched it too tight. While he was struggling with the knot, the double-ender's bow lurched into us two more times, splintering holes in our stern. Out of the corner of my eye I saw Pope with the knife. He jumped into the stern and cut through the towline. The foundering boat dropped behind us, wallowing broadside, and in a few seconds only the superstructure showed above the waves.

We stuffed the three jagged holes with rags and clothing and managed to deliver the three luckless fishermen to the scow. The one guy, the captain, held on to the marine radio, the only item salvaged. They had come up from the West Coast to fish Bristol Bay for the first, and probably last, time.

Freeman had cast off from the *Otter* after Pope had cut the swamped boat loose, so that we wouldn't have to pull his skiff along. He stayed close until we were near the scow, just in case. Before his visit to the *Otter*, he had delivered a skiffload, and now he would make another drift or two before the close of the period. A swamped boat wasn't that unusual in Bristol Bay, and there were fish to be caught, money to be made against the coming winter.

Because of our good deed and in consideration of the questionable shape we were in, the skipper of the scow let us tie off his stern to pick our fish, which we then delivered to him, all but the three hundred or so that were over the two thousand limit. One of the boats waiting in line to deliver was under the limit by more than three hundred, and we gave our surplus fish to them. Freeman should have hung around awhile longer. In any event, one good turn deserves another, and I think the Judge gave us credit for both that day, because the stuffing in the holes held well enough that the bilge pump could handle what leaked through, and we made it from the scow back over to the east side and the Naknek River.

Soon after we tied up to the cannery dock, the tide went out and we sat high and dry in the mud. The three holes could wait awhile to be mended. We needed to mend ourselves first with some rest. The unprecedented crew of the good ship *Otter* went to bed.

The rest of the season wasn't quite so dramatic or hectic, but the fishing continued first rate, and between us Steve and I made a good payday. Steve did as he pleased with his money; he had earned it. I presented my wife, back on the home farm, with a nice bonus check, which she happily applied to making much-needed improvements on the old house—as well as making improvements on her somewhat jaundiced view of the prospects of surviving in the woods on the proceeds of commercial salmon fishing. Carol was a brave and believing mate (despite the heavy sarcasm in her voice when she referred to me as "O Great White Leader"), but she had not imbibed the heady elixir of Adventure! as had I, and her feet were therefore planted much more firmly than mine on solid ground.

# 5

# THE DAY THE BOAT WENT DOWN

# AND ONLY ONE SURVIVED

The previous season (1965) with Pope, Teresa, and Steve on the *Otter* had been a banner year, but all the decisions, major and minor, about the when and how of fishing had been Pope's, as they had been VanDevere's the year before. I needed some hands-on experience making my own calculations and decisions out from under the umbrella of their guidance. That was my thinking through the winter back at Syracuse.

So I showed up in 1966 not only determined to fish *Port N Storm* again but this time without benefit of any experience other than my own as boat puller the previous two seasons. Two seasons might have been enough except that, as mentioned earlier, Pope and those pals of his I had met had been more inclined to teach me how to party than how to fish, and VanDevere, being the silent type, taught exclusively by example. As a consequence my learning the trade was at best hit-or-miss. There were any number of things serious fishermen discussed among themselves, such as where the fish were apt to be at any given time, the pros and cons of low-water or tide-rip or sandbar drifts, the latest advances in Fathometers, marine radios, bilge pumps, and so forth. But Pope and company never talked shop. Most of them had absorbed fishing lore along with their oatmeal and muktuk (blubber) from the earliest years and picked up on new developments effortlessly, almost without thinking. When they tied up after a fishing period they went uptown to one of the bars, and they didn't go to talk trade. If fishing came up at all it was usually in connection with some story, some joke, about what one or another of them had done or failed to do on this or that occasion.

Off the water I was still pals with Pope, and I had started to become friends with several of his gang, D Inn Crowd. It had happened slowly, without design. We would bump into one another on the dock or over beers at the Sea Inn, and I would see their dark eyes taking me in, since I kept coming back, sounding me out with their own kind of sonar. I think they raised their eyebrows and took notice that I was going to fish my own half-assed boat. A little bravery, even if foolhardy, earned some credit among men plying a dangerous trade. Especially so, and especially on the foolhardy side of the equation, when they heard that my partner would be a man with even less experience than I, with actually *no* experience—*none at all*. So to their minds the Professor had some balls; he was ready to go it alone, find out for himself. But mainly, I think, they came to regard me as one of their kind when I drank with them—drink, they knew, brought out the real man inside any possible calculated presentations. When I drank I never got loud or arrogant or nasty: quite the contrary. Like Pope, the more I drank the jollier I got and the readier I was for whatever. And then there was the night at the Sea Inn at the end of the season of '65 when this guy I didn't know at all for reasons unexplained had it in for me. Because I was an Outsider, a white man—and a professor to boot? Maybe. He watched me with curdled eyes under his high, spiky crewcut, and when I passed him to get another drink he swung around and wanted to know if I was a girl (my hair was pretty long—partly the hippie influence and mostly not getting to the barber), and I smiled and said, "That's right, I'm the Eskimo Queen and what are you, a porcupine?" He said, "I'll break your fucking jaw!" and I stopped and replied, "You'll shit

if you eat regular." At which point Kenny Brandon stepped between us, grinning, with his big back to the guy, and said, "Let
me buy you this one, Professor," and led me off. The hostile
dude had no ambition to challenge Brandon and just swung back
around and hunched over his drink. That sort of thing gradually
won the hearts of D Inn Crowd.

My partner that year was an old friend from New York, Bob
Henrie, a man who had never been aboard any vessel bigger
than a rowboat or caught anything bigger than a sunfish on any
water more threatening than a pond. Not only was he not an
experienced sailor or fisherman, he was a schoolteacher and
little-magazine poet, both activities far removed from the pragmatics of fishing salmon in Bristol Bay. That, of course, had been
my own case two years earlier, but pragmatics had never topped
my list of priorities, or his. The *poetry* of fishing, the splash and
dash of it, the adventure of it, and its ancient pedigree among
human beings—that's what drew Bob in. But there was about
him a rough-hewn quality not at all in keeping with the stereotype of the sensitive poet. A bit taller than I, he was built lean
and strong, broad-shouldered and tight-waisted. His wiry brown
hair came down low on his forehead, almost touching his bushy
eyebrows, from under which he regarded the world with intense
blue eyes, separated by a finely chiseled aquiline nose. In a
sou'wester he would look like someone right out of *Captains
Courageous*, perfectly typecast.

As the word wound its easy way around the Dillingham docks
that the Professor planned to fish *Port N Storm* with a New York
schoolteacher as boat puller, men who knew me a little would
see me and Bob coming along and offer something humorous
for our consideration, like, "How you doing, Professor? Gonna
try to commit suicide again this year?" Sometimes I might reply,
"Well, you know, if at first you don't succeed . . ." But usually I
just grinned and walked on by. Yet I knew there was some truth
to their jests. If we got caught too far out in a real blow, gale
force or better (or worse), it would be touch and go for us—

very likely touch bottom and go down. Okay, but I determined to exercise caution as well as muscle out there. We would run for shelter right off if a big blow came up. As strategy that plan had the virtue of simplicity: Cut and run. But it didn't work out that way the day the boats anchored in the safety of Clarks Slough heard through the crackling and buzzing of their marine radios that the converted sport-fishing boat with the straight sides had gone down, with only one survivor.

❖

*Port N Storm* was cruising around among the boats fishing off Clarks Point in clear view of the cannery buildings there on the bluff. I was listening on my old tube-type radio, wondering if and where we should lay out, because we hadn't seen much action in the nets we passed. This is known as radio fishing. Friends or family on different boats keep in touch with one another by radio. If one of them lucks into fish, he will try to let the others know so they can run over and get in on it. But of course he doesn't want the whole fleet bearing down on him (they would also be listening in), so he communicates in code of some kind, in a tone of bored understatement, because obviously he doesn't want to register excitement. Oh, hum, just one more idle fisherman waiting for the fish to show. Such a conversation might go like this:

"Ah, the *Wanda B*, the *Wanda B*, the *Bilikin Two*. You on, Kenny?" Click.

"*Wanda B* back. How's it going, Billy?" Click.

Instead of the more formal "over," and so forth, these low-key, apparently casual conversations used the click of the mike button to signal the end of a transmission. That way the communiqué could be fast and gone.

"Pretty slow, pretty slow. A kicker now and then, okay?" Click.

(A kicker is a fish that hits the net high, at the corkline, raising a fan of spray and shaking a shackle of corks with its struggles. Two or three low hits could be calculated for every kicker. So at this point an alert radio fisherman's ears would flip forward.)

"Yeah, well, I just made a water haul. How's your coffee situation?" Click.

"Got a fresh pot going." Click.

"Okay, sounds good. Where you at?" Click.

"East side, mile or so south of the needle's eye, okay?" Click.

"Roger, roger. I'm out." Click.

Translated, this conversation could mean that Kenny Brandon's brother Billy was into enough fish to warrant Kenny's pulling in his nets and heading southeast. The "needle's eye" was their code for a slot, a narrow passage, in the Long Sands bar running for miles down about the middle of Nushagak Bay. If you knew where the slot was, you could cut across the bar at certain stages of the tide instead of having to run down or up and around. Then again, maybe Billy was just scratching and waiting, and maybe Kenny was really going to join him for a cup of coffee. If an eavesdropping fisherman decided to pull and run to the spot he might not find it or he might find himself in a dead body of water listening to the guys back off Clarks Point, where he had been, getting excited because suddenly their nets were smoking. Radio fishing is chancy.

So I was cruising among the drifters, not hearing anything noteworthy on the radio, as we headed more or less down and out on the east side, toward Ekok. If Bob or I saw any hits or a bobbing corkline, we would find a spot of our own in the general area and lay out, making sure we left enough space between ourselves and the other boats. Fishermen respond badly when another boat lays out its nets between them and the incoming fish, thus intercepting them—a practice called "corking." One of the stories being passed around at the bars that season was how Big Harvey Samuelson, a leader among his people and a former Alaska Ranger, reacted when an Outside boat manned by Italians (locally referred to as dagos) corked him when he was on a productive drift. I enjoyed the story so much I put it into my "Ballad of Bristol Bay":

> *Well, Harvey got corked by a dago one day*
> *Turned loose his gear, towed the bastard away*
> *"Hey, what-a you do?" then the dago did say*
> *"Shut up," said ol' Harvey, "or I'll throw you in the bay"*

Then also, if you lay out too close to other boats, your nets— under the influence of a tide rip or varying rates of drift—might get tangled with another boat's nets, and if there are enough struggling fish in the webbing to sew them together, you have found hardship. At night and in rough weather it's a nightmare untangling the mess. Prominent in my memory bank was the night in '65 with Pope when our far shackle got meshed with that of another boat in choppy seas. Pope and I didn't realize it had happened until we heard shouts and made out the dim gray low-slung shape of a double-ender just off our port side. Two figures in the stern were pulling in and pointing astern. We made out the two end buoys close together and a triple row of corks. The shackles had meshed and their ends looped back on themselves: a triple threat. It was late, we hadn't slept after a long day, and I for one was already tired. I didn't feel kindly disposed toward Pope and his careless ways. We had to pull in the untangled portion of our net, picking the fish as we went, the two boats converging on the section of the nets the fish had stitched together, then try to tear the stitches apart, the two other guys and us yanking on our respective nets. Where we couldn't tear them apart, particularly where the mess had tripled, we had to lean way out to rip fish out of the webbing hanging between the two boats and then with all our strength haul as much of the tangled net aboard as we could manage and pick those fish, sometimes having to cut the webbing to get at them, all the while pitching and rolling and getting doused with spray.

There was no telling their nets from ours. So whose fish, theirs or ours? It was impossible to tell. The two guys on the other boat abreast of us now said nothing, which was what I said too. We were just struggling to get the nasty job over with. But Pope, as usual for him in such situations, was laughing and joking around—as far as I could tell, enjoying himself. "Here," he would say, tossing a fish into their hold. "This one must belong to you, it's got your name on it. But this one's ours, I'd know it anywhere." The two natives never responded. They just wanted to get free of the mess and away from the crazy white man.

So, with this scene in mind, I determined that when Bob and I laid out there would be a world of open water between us and the nearest boats.

After an hour or so of cruising around, we came up on a boat on the outer fringes of the pack whose corkline looked as if it had Saint Vitus dance, and at the same time Bob yelled, "Hey! A yumper! A yumper!" ("Yumper" was how some of the Scandinavians referred to a jumper, a salmon hurling itself clear of the water, a signal, since salmon run in groups, that fish were present.)

"Okay, Roberto," said I, "this is it. We found them." I estimated our slot and swung *Port N Storm* around to bring the wind astern. It pushed us along at a smart clip. Bob tossed the end buoy and lead line over the roller, and the net started peeling out, the corks *clop-clop*ping on the wooden slats of the roller. Bob kept watch as the lines uncoiled. Should one of them come off the pile in a tangle, it was his job as boat puller to dart forward and by grabbing the line in a certain way snap the tangle apart so that no kinks, which would reduce the fishable area of net, escaped into the water.

I was looking ahead when I heard him yell. As the Eskimo recognizes many different kinds of snow, the human ear distinguishes many kinds of yell. This one was different from the one Bob gave when he had spotted the jumper. This one was edged with astonishment and colored with panic. I swung around to see him pressed against the stern, his right arm stretched up over the roller, and instantaneously I realized his fingers were caught in the tightening webbing. The boat's forward momentum against the drag of the net already in the water had closed the mesh on his fingers like a vise. He was in danger of either losing his fingers or going over the roller with the net. In the second before I reacted, Bob's brilliantly blue eyes met mine with an expression of extreme concern. I threw the engine into reverse, the net slackened, and he yanked his hand free, minus the glove. It seemed he hadn't been quite fast enough in grabbing a kink in the lead line. To tell the truth, which I didn't tell him at the time, *Port N Storm* had been sailing ahead with the wind more than a little faster than was prudent. Operator problem.

To add to the excitement, just when Bob extracted his hand, a huge king salmon plowed into the last fathom of net off the bridle, bowing it out six feet or more, then bursting totally enmeshed up out of the water and backward over the corkline, where it hung, its struggles transmitting up the bridle and through the boat. It was the biggest king I had yet seen, probably close to a hundred pounds. The only reason our sockeye-size mesh held him was that his backward flip over the corkline had wrapped him in a bag of webbing.

Bob stared at the fish, then turned to me, his eyes as wide as they could get. "Jesus Christ!" he said. "If I'd gone over, it would have been just like Jonah and the whale. That fucking fish could have swallowed me whole."

I laughed, relieved that he was all right, his sense of humor intact. Fish were hitting high and low the length of the net, which couldn't be said to be smoking but was definitely puffing hard. I cut the engine and climbed back to the stern to stand with Bob, whose head was exploding from the combination of sudden events.

"There!" he cried, pointing. "Out by the buoy—three, four more of them! *Jesus Christ!*" He was shouting and grabbing my arm. "The kids won't believe this. I should have brought Billy up here." The big king struggled, hanging suspended in the web-bing a dozen feet from us. "Look at the *size* of that monster!"

This was the hottest action we had seen, and I didn't notice right away that we had drifted into an express lane. The tide was ebbing very fast, as the big tides do in Bristol Bay. Because of the tide rips, bars, and so forth, in some slots it moves out considerably faster than in others. By the time I looked up to get my bearings, we were the only boat around. In every direction, I saw nothing but water. Not another boat in sight. Uh-oh. Where had everybody gone? Did they know something I didn't? Had there been some warning about the weather? We hadn't listened to the radio since hitting into the fish. And, yes, it was in fact blowing much harder. To the south the sky had turned dark as a bruise. We had already drifted past Ekok Point and were down off the bluffs where the bay widens—and where there lurks in wait the notorious Ekok Tide Rip.

Tide rips are hospitable to fish but hostile to fishermen. When conditions of wind and tide so dictate, their animosity becomes pathological, homicidal. The water's behavior loses all rationality or predictability. You cannot read its mind because it has lost it. If it is frenetic elsewhere, in a tide rip it is insane. Waves come at you from any and every direction. There is no way you can play them, because they don't recognize any rules. Each wave is on its own, a quantum of elemental chaos. So we were not only caught out in a very considerable storm—the waves were beginning to blow their tops—but our little trollop of a boat had fallen into the maniacal clutches of the very Jack of all the tidal rippers.

The nets, all three of them, were tied off the stern cleat. Had I believed it possible to do without broaching and swamping, I would have switched ends, moved the bridle to the bow cleat, so that at least we would have been nosing into the waves, the nets acting as a sea anchor keeping the bow into the wind. Off the stern the nets still held us into the wind, but alas *Port N Storm*'s stern was square. Instead of slicing into the waves as the

Taoist bow would have done, playing them artfully, it fronted them squarely, as a square fronts life, head-on (even if ass backward), without give, toe-to-toe, slugging it out.

Pulling the nets aboard and running for Clarks Slough might have been a good idea an hour ago but was now impossible. The waves were too big. *Port N Storm* had neither a power roller nor stern controls to make it easier to get the nets in. Even if I started the engine and reversed to cut Bob a little slack, backing into the waves seemed likely to bring a big green one on board, more than our hand–bilge pump could handle. The strength of the wind and the weight of the loaded nets were too much for one man, anyway. All we could do, short of cutting the nets loose (a desperate measure), was to hang on and trust *Port N Storm* to ride it out, at least through the tide rip, hoping that in the meantime we weren't driven onto a bar.

I got cold and went below, but I didn't really calculate that we might drown (although just about anyone else would have). In fact I was chuckling because Bob looked so grim. He had always been the joker in the deck, the mad poet, the Zen lunatic, meeting the tempests of life with quips and quirks and a laugh. Now he looked—there on deck in black boots and slicker, the hood obscuring his face, his eyes a band of darkness beneath his collapsed brows—like a caricature of the Grim Reaper.

"Hey, Bob," I called, "come on down and warm up. You can't do any good up there."

He turned, looking very spectral, bending toward me. I couldn't see his eyes under the hood. He was saying something I couldn't make out. Then he reached up and undid his life vest from on top of the pilothouse and got into it, lurching around, trying to hold on and work the buckles at the same time. When he had managed it, he came down.

"Want me to get yours?" he asked, giving me a quick look.

"Oh, hey!" I laughed. "Things aren't that bad yet. We'll ride it out. But I tell you what, if we do go down, I want a nice hot meal in me. I'm gonna heat up some spaghetti."

"Shit, I hope you're right." Bob looked up at me from where he perched uneasily on the edge of the bunk, his blue eyes sober as judgment day. "I mean about riding it out. This is the shits. I feel like shit. As a matter of fact, I'm on the verge of shitting my pants right now."

That was the nearest to joking he got. I had left the radio on, though nothing was coming in clear, a lot of static and unintelligible voices sounding like a tape played backward. I think some of what we were hearing wafted over from the Nak-nek side, or maybe from Japan. It didn't sound like English, the little we could make out, and not really like Eskimo either. I was about to open the can of spaghetti when suddenly some fishermen, or probably scows, came through loud and clear.

"Yeah, one of those converted sport-fishing boats, you know, with the narrow beam and straight sides. They picked up only the one guy. The boat's cracked open on a bar."

Click.

Bob and I did just what they always do at such moments in the movies. We stared at each other.

"Yeah, okay, Nick. Did you get the name of the boat?"

"Ah, negative on that, Joe. They'll get all that from the survivor back at the cannery."

Click.

We continued to stare at each other, speechless as a couple of catatonics. But our minds were racing. Had we already gone down and was this some kind of postmortem time warp permitting us to hear the report of our deaths (*one* of our deaths)? Or were we under more stress than we realized? Was this the way it was in situations like this, men seeming normal but hearing things, having strange ESP flashes of the imminent future, as dying men are said to see their whole lives pass before them in instant replay?

As the scow was signing off and I was standing stock-still by the stove with the forgotten can of spaghetti in my hand, out of the corner of my eye I saw through the car window a very big wave coming astern. It blocked out the sky and raised the corkline as it came high as the back of a dinosaur rippling with power. The wave came on, bigger than any I had ever seen. Its top broke forward like a maniac's hair whipping into his eyes. Hissing and foaming at the mouth, it seemed literally intent on us, coming for us. It reared up above our little lady like a Tyrannosaurus rex and then lunged. But effortlessly, amazingly, and without the least trace of concern, *Port N Storm* simply rose to the occasion—rose precipitously and very high—and leapfrogged the monster.

Bob couldn't have seen the wave from where he was sitting, but he must have seen the expression on my face and felt the brute force heaving past. Without a word he reached into the bin for a pad and pencil and started writing. He was jotting down his last words, in case he was not the sole survivor—a message to his wife, with whom under normal circumstances he was at odds, and to his eight kids, from whom until now he had been glad to be away—confessing no doubt that he loved them all dearly. Green as he was (in more ways than one), he had a clearer sense of the danger we were in than I.

While he was writing, I went up on deck and worked my way back to the bilge pump. In passing, the wave had flung some of its wrath over the gunwale. As I pumped, I looked around. We were still in the rip heading down and out, and we were still, in all that roiling mass of gray water and sky, the only boat around: alone, all, all alone. But the waves, though whitecapping, did seem a little easier up ahead. If we could hang tough a while longer, we might soon slip out of the Ekok rip. Maybe then we could get the nets in and sneak back up to the slough. I hoped there weren't too many fish in the nets. If there were, we would have to cut the shackles loose after all. Too much weight in the stern, in this blow, would put us too low to the water. We would need all the freeboard we could get to make it to the slough. Better to lose a few bucks in fish and gear than fulfill the scow's prophecy of doom.

Back down in the cabin Bob remained on the edge of his bunk, his boots off but the orange life vest still over his black slicker. He had emptied the last of our booze (down the drain or down his gullet, he didn't say) and put his note in the bottle, the cap screwed back on. Then he sat there expressionless with the bottle in his hands. Maybe he figured that if they recovered his body the bottle might be found still clutched in a rigor-mortised hand and the note thus would get delivered. I didn't attempt a joke, and I never mentioned the message in the bottle afterward.

We found out later that a boat—a converted sport boat—had indeed swamped in the storm, with one man lost. We knew neither the boat nor the fishermen and learned only that they had come up from Bellingham to try their luck for the first time, two young men, very much like the crew of the swamped double-ender in '65. Every year some fishermen drown, and usu-ally several boats swamp. Commercial fishing is known to be one of the most dangerous of occupations. The sea will be itself. Precious life and horrible death are merely human notions.

After we drifted out of the tide rip we were able to haul in the nets, picking the fish as we went and throwing them up forward. We had to pull hard against the wind, hang on, and then haul in as fast as we could on the downward slide. I was glad there weren't all that many fish. What helped was the turn-ing of the tide, the interval of slack water. It took a long, bone-jarring time to reach Clarks Point. We found one of our scows moored in the lee of the point and managed to deliver our fish, although it was rough even there and a few more seams in our hull opened up from the banging we took against the scow's steel hull. The deckhands looked at us curiously, probably won-dering whether we were intrepid harvesters hungry for the bucks or, more likely, given the looks of us and our boat, a couple of greenhorns too dumb to know when to duck. But they said nothing. In Bristol Bay, as generally in outback Alaska, a man had license to commit any brand of folly he chose, no questions asked.

Clarks Slough, twisting inland, was thick with boats lying at anchor. In the twilight the curving line of all those boats with their mast and cabin lights flickering looked like a boulevard at night. The slough was cut deep by the perpetual tides, and the wind hummed in the exhaust pipes sticking up.

No one took notice of our arrival as we passed slowly among the boats. No close-up camera shots of faces at portholes breaking into smiles because by God we had made it, no slow-motion shots casting us into heroic proportions. Just the gray light of evening on the mute tundra, the slick gleam of the muddy banks, the wind whistling across the exhaust pipes. Any fisherman not sleeping minded his own business.

We found a spot and put out the anchor and went below out of the wind and lit the stove and sat awhile feeling the good warmth and the tension draining out of our bodies. We got out of the rain gear and, not bothering about food, slid into our bags. No telling how much sleep we would get before the engines starting up would wake us and we would move out with the fleet for another go at it.

That day had a disillusioning effect on Bob. It had been a little too real, in the way of mainstream reality, newspaper reality, which is to say grim reality. He couldn't find much poetry in it. Afterward the waters of Bristol Bay held no appeal for him. He looked at the sea askance now, as a man might look at a woman whom he no longer loved, incredulous that he ever had. But he stuck the season out, somewhat gloomily. We made "average boat," our catch about average for the fleet. That was good enough for me, a reassurance that I could do it on my own. Bob would go back home with some bucks in his pocket and a firm resolve in his mind:

*A man must be blind*
*To make up his mind*
*To go to sea once more*

As for me, I knew we had been in a bad situation—more accurately, in dire straits. But the knowledge was merely intellectual, abstract. Danger had been from the start simply an accepted part of the idea that drove me, and because of that a priori acceptance my emotions remained free of fear. "Be absolute for death;" counseled the duke in Shakespeare's *Measure for Measure*. "Either death or life shall thereby be the sweeter." So I had accepted death, absolutely, and thereby could respond to the beauty and wonder, the poetry of the sea, although in quiet moments alone with it, I have to say, I felt not only awe but also some dread. After all, the godhead nearly appears as itself in the sea, barely accommodated to our human frailty, and it was taught anciently in both East and West that no man can face undisguised godhead and live. Of course from another perspective—that of a cynic, say, a practitioner of the debunking approach to life—it could be said, as they say in Tierra del Fuego, that where ignorance is bliss, 'tis folly to be wise: I just didn't have sense enough to be scared and thus lucked out.

In any event I hadn't been warned off from fishing. The following season would find me once again flying to Bristol Bay to be partners with Gene Pope, just the two of us this time, Steve remaining with the family in New York, and Teresa remaining onshore, where it was warm and dry and safe.

The author standing on *Port N Storm* in 1964, the day he and VanDevere towed her to the dock off the North Kenai road for her launching into the voyage to Bristol Bay.   *Courtesy of Bob Durr*

The start of the journey to Bristol Bay. *Port N Storm* being lowered into Cook Inlet. *Courtesy of Bob Durr*

The PAF dock in Dillingham, looking toward the town.
*Foreground:* The old *Otter*'s bow and stern lines are looped around
the dock's pilings. *Port N Storm* is tied off the *Otter* and the other
boats in turn are tied off her and each other.   *Courtesy of Bob Durr*

Pope and the author *(left to right)* on *Port N Storm* in the small-
boat harbor at Dillingham, 1964, the day Pope came on board
with Teresa. Pope is wearing his sincere and innocent face.
*Courtesy of Bob Durr*

THE FISH
*Courtesy of Bob Durr*

A good shot of Gene Pope as Clark Kent. *Courtesy of Bob Durr*

Pope and the author pulling in the nets on the *Otter*, 1965, on the Naknek side. This must have been after the Big Run had passed through, because the nets aren't loaded. No bananas. *Courtesy of Bob Durr*

Pope as Captain Blood.
*Courtesy of Bob Durr*

The swamp double-ender the crew tried to save in 1965. With webbing in the prop, they couldn't make any headway with the swamped boat alongside, and right after this shot they dropped her back off the stern for towing, which was when she punched the three holes in the stern and they had to cut her. Down she went. *Courtesy of Bob Durr*

Teresa, The Professor, and Pope posing with a big king on the *Otter* in 1965. Steve took the photo. They were the unprecedented four-man crew on Naknek that year. *Courtesy of Bob Durr*

Drying nets at the end of the season after they had been hosed down, after which they would be bundled and hung in the net loft until next season.   *Courtesy of Bob Durr*

A painting by the author: salmon in fresh water ascending their natal stream to spawn and die. After entering fresh water, they quickly turn red and eventually grow hooked noses and big crooked teeth before dying in consummation of their life cycle. *Courtesy of Bob Durr*

The author's cabin on Back Lake.
*Courtesy of Bob Durr*

# 6

## HIGH BOAT

It had been a slow year so far, relatively few fish showing and a lot of boats looking: a bad combination. Catches had been small and spotty, a slug of reds here and there, but nothing steady, no flood of salmon up the bay. A lot of boats wouldn't even make expenses in a season like that. They would be operating in the red.

I was fishing with Genus Popieus that year, 1967, on his newly acquired boat, the *Diane*, a regulation gillnetter in good shape. She was built tough, a no-nonsense lady. There wasn't a frill or a smile anywhere about her. The only paint she wore was gray—everything, the hull, the superstructure, the controls, the bunks, a single tone of gray, as though they had just dipped her into a big paintpot. She was strictly a commercial enterprise, a stern apostle of America's faith that all you need is dough. But Pope, his name notwithstanding, wasn't at all religious about money. His standing there at the helm of such a sober and serious craft was a three-dimensional oxymoron.

Not wishing to trouble himself about finding fish or making decisions, he had insisted I be captain that year. He was sure I would enjoy the job. Cheechakos were like that, he knew. As for himself, he was into philosophizing. All appearances and behaviors to the contrary, he was a thoughtful, questioning man.

He saw me as an opportunity to get some things clear. And he was delighted to discover that in certain fundamental ways we thought alike. He would beam when I talked about how civilization was simply a huge mistake, an insane episode in our species' evolutionary career from which we might not escape alive. And when I told him how so many of the ancient sages who had awakened from the mass delusion consequently took to the woods and mountains, he would grin and see himself in their actions. He couldn't hear enough along those lines; it was like food and drink to him. Always it had seemed that he was just an oddball, a malcontent, a rebel without a cause or clue, a juvenile delinquent to the American dream everyone else adored but which for him had been a nightmare, back there as a teenager in Middle America. He had felt alone, odd man out, but he had stubbornly stuck with his gut feelings, the outlaw promptings of his nature. He would not toe the line. And now, as he saw it, here was a man, a professor no less, who told him the line wasn't worth toeing, that civilization and its discontents was a ten-thousand-year-old scam serving the interests of a handful of clever and ruthless maniacs skillfully mismanaging mankind's mind down through the generations to service their privileged lives at the cost of untold suffering and planetary destruction, a man who could call the names of great philosophers, poets, and seers to bear witness to the validity of Gene Pope's predilections.

So our fishing effort that year was almost no effort at all. We behaved like a pair of shiftless skunks. Instead of listening to the radio to learn where the fish were swimming, we listened to one another to learn what we were thinking. Instead of diligently testing for fish in different areas of the bay with short drifts using only one shackle, we just picked a nice open slot in one of the deepwater channels, laid out all our nets, and rode the tide back and forth while we drank coffee and smoked cigarettes and philosophized.

The kind of philosophy, or metaphysics, we talked had

mainly to do with the laws of nature and the right conduct of life in keeping with those laws. So we got into the Chinese idea of the Tao, which Pope hadn't come across before, and espe-cially we talked about the Taoist principle of *wu-wei*, of going along with life in an attentive but relaxed way, without striving, without tiring yourself out trying to impose your will on it, just watching it and leaving it to its own spontaneities. We didn't talk about supernatural happenings, miracles and the like—what I called the spooky stuff. But it was at least surprising, and per-haps strange, that by the end of the season we were ranked seventh highest boat in numbers of fish caught, when we hadn't even really tried. We didn't take it as anything more than "luck": The incalculable network of events, of which we were a part, had simply placed us in the right spot at the right time. Certainly we didn't think of it as an instance of the spooky stuff, though maybe it had something to do with *wu-wei*. Nonstriving was our style that summer, and this much can be said: It worked for us.

❖

Mainly just two drifts, the one pure "luck" and the other a nice blend of luck and pluck, were responsible for placing us among the highliners. Apparently the currents of circumstance follow their own mysterious channels, and if a miss is as good as a mile, then nothing succeeds like success. We caught a lot of fish in the 1967 season.

The day we made the first big catch was flat calm, sunny and hot, a chrome yellow day. The bay was as placid and smooth as a bowl of lemon-lime Jell-O. As usual, Pope and I were off by ourselves, cruising around in an area void of other boats. There were no other fishermen around because there had been no re-ports and no reason to suppose that it was an area worth being in. As the day was fine and balmy and the living easy, we were less inclined than ever to hurry on over to the other side where the general fleet was congregated because someone had caught a few fish. We had listened in enough to know that not much was happening. So we removed our shirts to soak up more of the precious sun and continued our discussion of the Tao as we sailed along under the benign skies. Overhead the gulls, brilliantly white in the sunlight, rode the currents of air without effort.

"So the idea of this *wu-wei*," Pope was saying, testing his understanding and trying to relate it to himself, "is to just take it easy—happy-go-lucky?"

While Gene Pope had never been called diligent or ambitious, he had on occasion, as mentioned, been called other things less complimentary, among them lazy and shiftless—or happy-go-lucky, if the name-caller had been kindly disposed. Pope never protested, waved it off with a laugh, but I suspect public opinion nevertheless sometimes smarted. Now, however, he was beginning to understand that the truth of the matter of his "shiftlessness" might be quite other than what public opinion maintained. If his freewheeling way with life was really in accord with an ancient wisdom that regarded spontaneity as the way of nature itself and nonstriving as the modus operandi of the wise man, well, then, the pejoratives "lazy" and "shiftless" were probably nothing but the badmouthing of ignorant, anal-retentive types who had voted themselves into positions of moral superiority simply by virtue of their numerical superiority. Gene Pope had been maligned by a world of uptight assholes.

"Taking it easy, yes," I said, "following the path of least resistance, like water. Going with gravity. Right." Pope was listening very closely. His industry might be slow, but his intelligence was quick. In his mind the shoe fit. The path of least resistance was the way he liked to go.

"But," I went on, "there's a world of difference between the man in harmony with the Tao and the ordinary happy-go-lucky guy."

I paused for a puff of my cigarette and another sip of coffee.

"Well, like what?" Pope wanted to know. He was impatient, anticipating that his gold star was about to be placed in escrow.

"The man aware that the Tao is living his life is alert, very sensitive to the flow of events his life floats in. He has what Keats called 'Negative Capability,' by which he meant the ability to stay loose in the middle of ambiguities and uncertainties, without closing things down with stock responses and mental abstractions or substituting the map for the territory. But the happy-go-lucky guy typically is just the opposite—easy because his map is carved in stone: He's swallowed the conventional wisdom whole and thinks he's got it all figured out. He's a case of Keats's 'egotistical sublime'—the smugness of the hard-core ego. And that's just the *opposite* of open awareness. He's not with the watery Tao, he's fixed comfortably in place like a rock. He doesn't flow with the currents of life."

Pope's face had clouded over during the course of this dissertation. He glanced up at me over his coffee, and I caught a flash of his demon whipping its tail in agitation, and I knew that my fine distinctions didn't matter: Pope would be Pope no matter what I or the world made of him. Somewhere, in the nuclei of his cells, he knew he had the ultimate authority to be himself. I was about to assure him that I didn't mean to be seeming to label him "happy-go-lucky"—that I knew he was much more than that—when suddenly the calm of the listless water was shattered by the silver bullet of a leaping salmon off our port bow. Then another, and another. They shot up right out of the water, iridescent in the sunlight, and dived back in headfirst. There were jumpers all around us, the water rippling with interlocking circles like a pond at the start of a heavy rain.

"Wo-ho-ho!" said Pope. "What have we here?" ("Wo-ho-ho" wasn't his usual exclamation, and I wondered if the Chinese terms in our conversation had influenced his choice of syllables.)

He was laughing as he leaped back into the stern. He grabbed the end buoy and lead line and turned to me.

"What say, Captain, shall we catch us some fish?"

I throttled way down and looked swiftly around. Not another boat in sight. We owned these fish uncontested. We could lay out wherever and whenever we chose.

"Heave-ho, matey," I replied, and over the roller went the buoy and the lead line.

Fish started hitting immediately as the net strung out behind us. We had lucked into a school of salmon playing around. We were right in the middle of a nice big slug of fish. The nets weren't about to smoke, but the action was fast and steady.

Earlier we had noticed Johnny Larson's boat a couple of miles east and above us, off by itself, as was typical of Johnny, who played the fishing game like solitaire. But he was one of D Inn Crowd, a brother, and that was all the reason Pope needed to want to cut him in on our good luck. He went below and chuckled when he raised Johnny on the radio.

"Hey, Johnny, you got a little free time? Feeling bored? Well, here's a suggestion: Get the lead out of your ass and come on over and join our little party! There's some sexy dancing girls jumping around all over the place."

The message was obvious enough.

"Where you guys at, Gene?"

Pope gave him a brief description, enough so he would spot us in the area—the only boat around. Other fishermen might also get the message, of course, but they were too far off to reach us before the main course would be over: They would have to take the leavings, if any. But it was typical of Pope's careless and liberal nature that he would want to share his good luck with a buddy. It wouldn't occur to him to hog it for himself. He wasn't well adapted to modern times.

We learned a few days later that we were high boat for that period.

❁

The second time that season we hit into them good wasn't as pleasant or easy as the first. It was a blustery day, wind and spasmodic rain frothing the water, the veiled sun gleaming through the roiling clouds now and then, casting a cold, comfortless sheen over everything.

We had ridden the ebb right on down the middle channel and were now almost to the outside marker. Once again we were the only boat around. Everyone was crowded together up near Clarks Point, where a few fish had been reported. Now the tide was turning, and we were faced with the need to make a decision: Should we continue our dissolute ways and just leave the nets in the water? They would get a good washing and keep us comfortably in line with wind and wave. We could fix another pot of coffee and drift back on up while we philosophized. Or should we haul in the nets like serious fishermen and run back up to scratch with the others?

We stood together by the wheel, bundled in sweaters and rain gear, smoking cigarettes and sipping coffee, as was our wont, discussing our options as we gazed astern at the waves breaking along the corkline. Then, at about the middle of the first net from the boat, a whole fathom of the line bowed out, quivering, and a couple of salmon burst out of the water wrapped in the webbing and arced back over the line, taking the net with them.

"That's a *slug* of them!" Pope pulled the butt from his mouth and tossed it over the side. "And they ain't traveling alone."

Other geysers fanned up along the line. *Biff, biff, biff.* We were into the fish again, and not another boat in sight. A little Zen saying popped into my mind: "Sitting quietly, doing nothing, spring comes, and the flowers grow all by themselves." In a universe outside time, where everything is laid out eternally and merely unfolding sequentially before our eyes, why wear yourself out struggling with hard decisions? Just pay attention and see what's in store for you.

"Good," Pope was saying, synchronous with my thoughts. "Now we don't have to make up our minds what to do." He turned to me with his tight-lipped grin. "How about another cup of coffee, Captain?"

Naturally we just left our nets in the water, where the fish had come to them.

The action slowed down after the first slugs, but the hits continued up and down the line at a steady pace. And it could be better than it appeared if most of the fish were hitting deep instead of at the corkline where we could see them. We could be loading up pretty good.

But the wind was picking up with the flood, here and there white-capping the bigger waves. We were starting to drift pretty fast. Earlier that day while drifting down with the ebb we had watched a line of breakers emerge along the sandbar that ran half the length of the bay between channels. Sandbars were often good fishing, but they made me nervous. If you were careless enough to let one grab you during a blow it could grind your boat and you into debris. Turnabout may be fair play, but I wasn't into becoming food for fishes. I wasn't interested in a sandbar drift, but the chance to make a big catch in a generally bum year would be tempting to many a fisherman. Personally, in this instance, as noted, I wasn't tempted at all, but I anticipated that my adventurous partner might be.

"Well, shit," I said, watching our approach to the breakers, "just when we're into them pretty good we have to pull in."

"Maybe not," Pope responded, adopting a reasonable, thoughtful stance and wearing his serious and sincere look. "If we can ride it out till the bar is under, we might be able to sneak across."

Uh-oh. Uh-oh—more Popean fun and games, playing hide-and-seek with the Grim Reaper. Though I was wary, hesitant, the leaven of Adventure! was apparently still fermenting my brain into a light and easy readiness. And we were catching fish, in a year when it looked like we might not even make expenses.

"Sure," I agreed. "We'll leave out only the one shackle and watch the situation. If it looks like we're going to bump the bar, we can pull in fast and get out of there."

"Begging the captain's pardon," Pope demurred, wearing the

sad and reluctant expression of a bearer of ill tidings. "But they're not hitting hard enough to make this kind of sandbar drift worth the trouble for what only one shackle can hold."

Aha! Three shackles then, no doubt he recommends. Not so easy or fast getting three shackles back into the boat as just one. I looked at him and noted the twinkle in his eye. Of course Pope almost always had a twinkle in his eye, but in this one I caught a glimpse of my partner curious to see what his philosophical friend would do. I knew all too well that Pope had a propensity for risky business. He liked it that way. But in this instance, for myself, was the risk worth the possible reward? I hesitated, thinking it over.

"Take no thought . . . ," he murmured. He was reminding me of one of my favorite texts, implying that here was an opportunity to act on my advocacy of the unpremeditated life. I could have come right back at him with, "Tempt not the Lord thy God," but I did want those fish; and if caution had been my game I wouldn't have been there in Bristol Bay with Gene Pope in the first place. I would have been safe in my tenured bunker at Syracuse.

"Sounds good to me," I said.

Pope grinned.

But it was clear that we were moving toward the bar too fast to hold the drift until the flood covered the exposed sands with enough water for us and our nets to scrape across. The wind was too strong, pushing the sternward boat like a sail, and instead of heading up the channel, we were being driven up and across toward the bar. I ran these observations by Pope, and he nodded.

"If the captain pleases," he said, "I'll hang the bridle off the bow so the wind can't push us so hard, and not only that but with the nets away from the prop we can use the engine to push back a little."

He beamed at me with the burlesqued look of a subservient person thrilled to have offered a clever suggestion to a higher authority. I ignored the burlesque but went for the suggestion.

Actually, he was letting me know how we might be able to hang on to this drift. Had I objected to this plan or the three-shackle idea, he would have backed off readily and gone along with whatever I thought best. He really didn't care one way or the other. He wasn't into catching fish so much as catching my scent, sniffing me out from among the heady scent of my words. Being sure about life, his own life, was more important to him than the possibility of being a few dollars less poor the following winter.

Handling the lines was mainly the boat puller's job, as Pope knew—a fair trade, in his view, to exchange the troublesome matter of making decisions for the simple matter of manual manipulations that left his mind free to muse. This division of labor wasn't absolute, especially if the partners were friends. The captain would often handle the lines, and his partner would often help make decisions. In this instance Pope did everything but agree to his own plan: I did that.

The plan seemed worth a try. After moving the nets from the stern to the bow, we would throttle forward enough to put slack in the bridle, so that the boat wouldn't be functioning as a sail dragging the nets toward the bar. When there was just the right amount of slack in the bridle, and before risking overrunning the net, we would throw the engine into neutral, drifting back again until the bridle straightened, then repeat the maneuver, all the while gauging our position with the bar and trying to estimate when there might be enough water to gently bounce over it and into the channel on the other side. It looked feasible on paper. Pope demonstrated a few times, always nosing to starboard of the bridle, downstream of the tide. Then he moved aside to let me, the captain, take over. He lit a cigarette and stood watching for a while. Then, without explanation, he turned to go below.

"Give me a shout when we're across," he said as he ducked through the doorway.

Whoa! Was this tactic so assured of success that he could

take a nap? It didn't seem that way to me. But the fact was that he was gone and I was in charge. I alone would judge whether we were or were not a safe distance from the breakers, and if not, whether I had calculated enough time for us to pull in the nets—with who knew how many fish in them—before those curled waves like giant fists started pounding us against the hard-packed sands. That was my job. I was the captain, you see.

Maybe by this gesture of going below Pope was expressing his confidence in me. Or maybe this whole maneuver was really a foregone conclusion, no more than a matter of putting in the time. Maybe he had done it a hundred times before. But then again maybe this was another one of his tests or tutorings—a kind of off-the-end-of-the-dock swimming instruction, with the instructor confident he could pluck me out of the water before I drowned. What was certain was that I was alone with the wheel and myself, the nets roller-coastering up forward and the breakers committing hara-kiri astern. That was all there was in my life now, the wind and its minion waves coming at me and the breakers behind me and the faithful Chrysler moving the plunging, buoyant boat forward, pulling the bridle in an arc back on itself till the corks were right there below me on the port side, and then flipping into neutral and dropping back slowly until we were about to tighten on the net, then into forward again—not too much throttle, don't want to run over the net and snag it on the skeg—taking the bridle abreast of the first corks again, and all the time watching the individual waves, keeping our nose into them. This was where I was at, this was the point present of all my days, the focused consummation of everything I was or did or that had happened to me. It became hypnotic—staring at the whitecapped waves endlessly rolling toward me along the rippling net, with always a fan or two of spray from hits somewhere along its length, throttling slowly forward, dipping into the troughs, rising up on the crests, then dropping back in neutral, then forward again, over and over, until I lost track of time and there was no other me than the one watching the waves and working the boat, turning to gauge the status of the bar with cool awareness and without a trace of fear, purely concentrated on the work at hand.

Pope remained below. I really couldn't imagine him nervously peering out a porthole. Probably he was musing or daydreaming on his bunk. Good. That was fine with me. Let him stay below. What mattered was reading each wave and working the throttle and keeping track of the sandbar. Pope was below, I was at the wheel. That's how it was.

I can't say whether I actually coolly assessed the situation and took a deliberate guess, risking enough water under us to drift over the bar, or had just spaced out, entering another consciousness that picked up signals without translating them into distinct ideas, but there was Pope standing next to me.

"Well, I see we're across," he said. He beamed at me with his exaggerated smile.

That we had crossed the bar was news to me. Good news, but nevertheless news. I hadn't been aware that we had crossed. All I had known was that the water we had been drifting toward at any given time looked okay, and so I had just kept at it. Apparently that was all I had needed to know.

We were high boat for that period, too. A little applied *wu-wei* on the waters of Bristol Bay, perhaps.

❀

The season of '67 was significant for more reasons than our achieving high-boat status. It was in many ways a watershed for me in Bristol Bay, because by the end of that summer there remained no question that I had become a member in good standing of Dillingham's elite—which is to say most notorious—fishermen. I was not only invited to sit on the board of directors of D Inn Crowd, but because of my obvious qualifications as a professor of English they made me secretary. But as always with this wild bunch, it was my behavior in the course of the two-day bash featuring the celebrated Love-in Girl that erased all residue of doubt from their minds and hearts that I was indeed of sufficient stature as a reprobate to deserve anointment.

# 7

# TWO DAYS OF THE LOVE-IN GIRL

Pope and I were just hanging out that day, lounging around on deck in the heat of the afternoon sun, our shirts off, not even talking much, our energies as aimless as flotsam and jetsam at low-water slack. Waiting for the tide in the affairs of fishermen to turn. We were at the same time itchy, suffering a mild case of red ass: bored yet restless, standing still but wanting to go— a condition something like cabin fever or the malaise men experience in combat situations when, after the sharp excitement of a firefight, they have to dig in and wait. Fishing was like war in that respect, the fish suddenly showing, the hustle and fever of the catch, the element of danger in heavy seas, and then the shutdown of the closed periods and the spillover restlessness. All of which probably has something to do with the fisherman's propensity for hard drinking and partying, even more than is true of the generality of Alaskans, which is true enough.

We had been idle for almost a week. The entire fleet had been beached to let enough salmon sneak through to ensure a future crop. We understood that. We didn't resent Fish and Game's mandate per se. What nettled us as we lay idle was that the Japanese high-seas fleet would be out there reaping a disproportionate share of the harvest at our expense.

*Come the Fourth of July and the Big Run is here*
*Open up a jug and a case of beer*
*Sit on the beach boys and take your ease*
*Fish and Game needs escapement for the Japanese*

During these closed periods, if you were diligent and seriously into making money, you put your restlessness to good use by mending your nets, caulking your hull, fine-tuning your carburetor, and so forth. But if you were shiftless (inclined to the pleasure principle) and not all that much into money (the reality principle), you dissipated your excess energies at the Sea Inn Bar or the Willow Tree Inn, anticipating that something wondrous would happen. And usually it did, if you hung on long enough for your chemistry to change. Everything is known in the mode of the knower. If the knower's mode becomes disassociated from care and common sense and passes over into carelessness and euphoria, everything then assumes the potential to become wondrous. Of course, everything also has a price, especially chemically induced euphoria, but we lived on credit, believed in deficits, and never worried about paying the bill until it arrived. Most humans need a shot of euphoria on occasion, never mind the cost. We don't live by bread alone, but also by wonder. Socrates said that philosophy begins and ends in wonder, and by that reckoning D Inn Crowd was a fraternity of philosophers. They were, unbeknownst to themselves, seekers after ecstasy, the primal state of being that has been squelched in us by the conditioning process called civilization. The sop they threw to the dismal dog guarding the portals of the wondrous was soaked in booze, the only "psychedelic" they knew. They weren't students of poetry, but when, under the appropriate stimulation, I would recite these lines from A. E. Housman, they had no difficulty understanding what he meant:

*Could man be drunk for ever*
*With liquor, love, or fights,*

*Lief should I rouse at morning*
*And lief lie down at nights.*

*But men at whiles are sober*
*And think by fits and starts.*
*And if they think, they fasten*
*Their hands upon their hearts.*

So Pope and I, being sober, were standing there drinking coffee and smoking cigarettes, idly watching the wind flashing through the clumped grass along the cutbank above our heads, the tide out, the *Diane* sitting stolidly in the mud of the small-boat harbor, and I at least was indeed thinking in fits and starts, about the beluga meshes in our gear and the temperamental bilge pump that functioned only when so inclined and how I'd like to come out a little in the black this year instead of black and blue, when a voice from above blew in on the wind calling our names.

"Pope! Professor! What the *fuck* are you doing down there when there's a love-in going on? You're missing *the Love-in Girl!*"

This was the summer of 1967, and by then everyone in the lower forty-eight was familiar with the term "love-in" and the idealistic philosophy it implied: Make love, not war. Because, the argument went, making love is a lot healthier and a lot more fun than making war, and because the anal-retentive types who prefer war to love are very often victims of the social disorder known as lackanookie, it follows as the night the day that making love a lot more and a lot better must go a long way toward curing the malady of repressed horniness afflicting mankind periodically in the form of war. You don't need more money, more power, more hatred: All you need is love. But this was Alaska's Bristol Bay, port of Dillingham, a region far removed from cultural centers and cultural revolutions. Its young people had just recently caught up with Elvis. No flower children had yet blossomed on the scene. If "love-in" didn't register as a perfect blank in the minds of Dillingham's indigenous fisherfolk, it translated as something like "gang-bang."

We lifted our eyes in the direction from which the voice had come just as the slickly dark head of Freeman Roberts rose out of the undulating grass like Poseidon rising from the waves, in an early Elvis hairdo.

"She's wearing a loose shirt, complete with nipples, and a miniskirt and not much else. Even her feet are bare. She's a looker and she's doing some kind of weird dance all over the Sea Inn and babbling about a universal love-in, whatever the fuck *that* means. Tits and ass, boys, tits and ass."

With that he was gone. Back, presumably, to the Sea Inn Bar and the Love-in Girl, having done his brotherly duty by informing the delinquent Pope and the Professor.

We looked at one another: I, the university professor who had witnessed the emergence of the counterculture, with a sly surmise—the hippie advance guard had finally arrived—and Pope, the cultural dropout and backwoods predator, with the brightening sense that some kind of game was afoot.

"What indeed," said Pope, thrusting out his jaw, "are we doing down here?"

Not given to speculation or procrastination, he was over the side and up the cutbank, legs churning. With me close behind.

But of course when we reached the Sea Inn she was gone.

Yet her aura lingered on like the ghost of a strange and memorable event. As we stepped out of the sunlight into the perpetual gloaming of the Sea Inn, we made out a cluster of familiar forms at the bar. The rest of the place was empty. The blinds were drawn. There was a conspiratorial intensity about those figures huddled in the dim light, an air of excitement that belied their postures of macho cool. There was something odd about the way they fell silent and turned toward the door when we entered. Also, not only were they clustered together around Frank (Frank Tomalson, manager of the Sea Inn, a very large, barrel-chested man with a big nose and permanently fierce eyes), but they were passing around a bottle of tequila, with lemon and salt. This was not usual. Something had definitely gone down there that day.

As we approached, Freeman grabbed the bottle and thrust it toward us.

"It's tequila time!" he cried in a voice loud enough to be suspect. This was obviously not his first nor very likely his second or third tequila time. It was also not to be his last.

Frank glared down at us in a friendly welcoming way. "You two got here just in time," he said. "This is now a private party." He walked around the end of the bar, went over to the door and locked it, then came back and filled the shot glasses again, banging two more down for Pope and the Professor.

Apparently this select company of Dillingham's finest was in the process of trying to determine exactly what had happened there that afternoon, or at any rate what it meant. And just as Native Americans in former times prepared themselves for the consideration of weighty matters by relaxing mind and body in the sweat bath, so did these latter-day savages prepare themselves with the infusion of sufficient doses of firewater, the elixir of which, rising like steam, warmed and stimulated the right side of their brains and simultaneously charged their breasts with the courage to perform deeds of derring-do.

Tequila time went like this: Each man had a shot glass, a couple of wedges of lemon, and a salt shaker in front of him. Someone would yell, *"Tequila time!"* and Frank would pour while they each licked and then salted the area between thumb and forefinger on their left hand. Then the line of men, with a rhythmic synchronization reminiscent of the Rockettes, licked the salt, sucked the lemon, downed the shot, and slammed the glass back onto the bar.

In this fashion the story of the Love-in Girl was pieced together, bit by bit, which was how it remained in their minds, like particles in colloidal suspension, never to attain coherent form.

By now the world had begun to change. Time past and time future, with their attendant baggage, were dropping away, leaving only time present, the moment at hand, which had become larger, more colorful, more carefree and alive, more wondrous and open-ended to unimaginable possibilities. Tequila time had transported them out of time: They were now living in the present tense.

*Yes sirree, she surer than shit had been there. Yeah, miniskirt and all.* "And all" meaning long brown legs, California tanned, and bare feet, and what's more, Freeman swears, bare-assed, and what's more, too, Kenny adds, no bra, no bra at all. She pops up out of nowhere and starts doing this fluky dance when the Scott McKenzie number about coming to, or in, San Francisco with flowers in your hair begins on the jukebox. She's smiling and waving her arms and mumbling with half-closed eyes about this universal love-in and how we can change the world, rearrange the world, like she's in some kind of trance, and all the guys watching look like they've fallen into a trance, too.

Pope slams his fist down on the bar, making all the glasses jump to. "I'd like to know what she's been drinking!" he declares.

And I'd like to know what she's *on*, thinks the Professor, looking savvy.

"Well, she didn't get it here," says Frank, glaring directly at Pope, eyes bulging, eyebrows raised to his hairline, looking as though he had just said, "Maybe you'd rather have my number twelve shoved down your throat," which was his boilerplate for any drunk fisherman objecting to being cut off. It was just Frank's way. He had had to be so tough so young he didn't know how else to come on. Actually, he was fond of Pope and the Professor.

As far as the Professor can figure it, reading between the broken lines of the data offered up for interpretation, the Love-in Girl is a California hippie on summer vacation from college, intoxicated with the good news of love and freedom (which,

conjugated, form free love) and the exuberant influence of the
ganja guru, with very possibly the aid and abetment of a little
Owsley acid. She had come to Alaska with a guy, they had split,
she had run into a fisherman in Anchorage who counseled her
to go to Bristol Bay for the real Alaska and the real Alaskans,
even real Eskimo. So she is here to soak up the real thing and
no doubt to preach the gospel of love and freedom. In the minds
of my colleagues, however, she sizes up as a wacky but nevertheless good-looking and wildly sexy broad up for grabs.

So we are ready some time later to sally forth in quest of the
fabulous Love-in Girl. Protected as we are by the dimension of
adventure, romance, mirth, and comaraderie as by shining ar-
mor, we feel fully qualified to tilt with dragons, windmills, or
whatever strange enchantment had whisked her away from our
solicitations. Or, put otherwise, we feel invulnerable to the
slings and arrows of mundane reality because we are enveloped,
as Galahad in his dauntless faith, so we in the magical mantle
of our inability to attend to anything but the world at the immediate end of our noses, nor to experience that world as anything more or less than a collage of incomprehensible wonders.

"I wonder," says the Professor, stopping suddenly, for he and
Pope have been sallying on down the road with, as far as the
Professor is aware, no idea at all as to where they are headed.
The other seekers have vanished, apparently beamed up. "I won-
der," the Professor says, "where she is."

Pope looks back from a few paces ahead, where his momentum has carried him, bright-eyed and bushy-tailed as always.

"Fuck!" he bellows, shooting his finger out at the Professor.
"We'll find her! To the victor belong the spoils!"

Pope's voice is awesome in its magnitude. It seems to reach
the Professor as a palpable force, and he totters backward a step
or two. He thinks he sees a light in one house go on and a light
in another go out. He thinks he hears a tinkling sound like
breaking glass. A door flies open in the little white house they
are nearest to, and out steps Freeman Roberts, with Kenny Bran-

don and his partner, Louie Hereshka (looking like a cross between Edward G. Robinson and Jack Palance), and behind him
Jerry Nicholson (another D Inn Crowd brother, looking like a
black-haired version of Alan Ladd in *This Gun for Hire*), one
behind the other, the file of them reminding the Professor of a
Warhol painting of Presley, Elvis upon Elvis arising: the upswept
dark hair, the sultry air, the shirttails tucked into belly buttons,
the supercilious eyebrows struggling ineffectually to fully raise
the eyelids, so weighted with cool are they. They have heard
Pope's barbaric yawp and have come forth to bring their brothers' inestimable presences among them.

Pope and the Professor have stumbled upon a cabin party,
which in Bristol Bay is a kind of cocktail composed of one part
booze, one part people with personalities famous among the bars,
and one part freewheeling anticipations, with sex and violence
the bitters.

So back into the little white house they all go. And sure
enough she had been there, briefly but with impact. The galaxy
of stars in attendance was formed out of the whirl of her passing
and now awaits her imminent return. How she was found and
by whom the Professor never learns, nor does he try to find out.
What would it matter anyway. Water under the bridge. With
mind and eyes pleasantly disengaged from the reality principle,
he looks around. As the eye is, such the object. So other eyes
might have seen things differently.

Kenny, eyebrows raised, sits next to a native beauty, whose
bright eyes and teeth flashing among her whistles and bows give
her the look of a jack-o-lantern painted like an Easter egg, and
whose big black hair looping and spiraling around her pretty
face like the serpents of Medusa seems a foreshadowing of Dolly
Parton, and as such, fit complement to Kenny, whose own hair
looms in ebony grandeur above his forehead. Greasy kid's stuff,
maybe, but evidently too slick for that old put-down, gravity.
Freeman sits on his other side next to a cute and wide-eyed
little bunny who appears just barely old enough to be at this

movie and is obviously thrilled to be touching thighs with the handsome and renowned Freeman Roberts. His frontal wave rising out of his scalp like a tsunami is just as impressive as Kenny's—maybe more so—but the chiseled mass of Freeman's jutting chin has the effect of balancing it out, and moreover conveying the assurance that should worse come to worst and the great black wave collapse, it would at least crash splendidly among the rocks and not just topple over into empty space.

The Nicholson brothers are there too, Jerry the Chaplain ("the Chaplain" because he's the most irreverent) and Bobby the Asiatic Throwback, as he was wont to refer to himself and our native pals: "What do you think of us Asiatic throwbacks, Professor?" The Professor notices that Bobby wears the kind of patent-leather shoes Wall Street brokers once wore, but no socks. Bobby's crewcut hair stands up in three-inch spikes as though he were in a perpetual fright, but his eyes have the kind of sloe shape and mocking expression another Nicholson was to make famous.

They are all seated on an overlong, overstuffed sofa passing a jug back and forth. In the kitchen some other people the Professor doesn't know are sharing another bottle. All present are in various stages of drunk. One stage of which is unconsciousness: in which, unknown to anyone but his wife and Kenny, the resident Tiger lies quietly and, for a while, harmlessly in the tiny bedroom just off the living room. "Tiger" in Bristol Bay is not a nickname lightly given but a title richly earned. It is a designation conferred upon a select few fishermen noted not only for uncommon physical strength and toughness, nurtured by a hard life on the fish boats and traplines, but for a fortunately uncommon propensity to exercise that brute force in extreme and uncontrolled violence at the least and most unpredictable provocation. Tigers don't just engage in fisticuffs, they bash in noses, dig out eyes, knock out teeth, bite off ears, break arms or legs or ribs or jaws, as in real life. They put adversaries into hospitals and, occasionally, cemeteries. That justice consequently usually triumphs and rids society of this one menace is nice but of no comfort to the recently defunct.

Dark Dolly, as the Professor later came to think of her, Dark Dolly—flirting with Kenny, who sits perched on the edge of the couch laughing and nodding constantly, nervously, looking a little hyper, like a runner before the gun goes off—Dark Dolly, turned toward Kenny, smiling warmly, her hand on his knee, is, alas, the Tiger's wife.

It is knowledge of the Tiger's dormant presence smoldering in the next room that causes Kenny to experience a certain intermittent sense of urgency whenever the balloon of his high deflates momentarily at the prick of reason, only to puff back up on course at the next laugh. This is not to imply that Kenny has no macho. On the contrary, having spent the normal portion of his life at macho movies as a true believer, if push comes to shove he will fight. But until then, until his blood is aroused, being basically a good-natured guy, he'd rather not—especially not with some pitiable maniac whose mind when drunk becomes a pool of blind resentment and hate waiting for an opportune object on which to void itself. Kenny has no wish to become that object, and he'll take any honorable means to avoid the possibility. When he is drinking, however, and getting farther and farther removed from the cautious voice of reason listing probabilities and consequences, he will eventually arrive at the place where he doesn't give a shit and certainly won't take any, Tiger or no Tiger. And Dark Dolly certainly is pretty.

When suddenly there she is again—the Love-in Girl. She appears to be escorted by one of Fish and Game's bearded scouts, all corduroy and plaid, feeling out of place and smiling hesitantly. And she is certainly a looker, or so it seems to the Professor. He sees at once that whatever she has been on is still charging her battery, whether grass or acid or maybe just her instant celebrity status. She is talking, laughing, gesturing nonstop, wearing baggy slacks now (but not so baggy that you can't tell that she's nicely rounded) and a man's loose shirt open a few buttons down revealing firm-as-Jell-O little jiggles as she moves, testifying that she indeed wears no bra. Long brown hair parted in the middle, no makeup, a necklace made of seeds around her neck. The Professor sizes her up knowingly: a hippie chick, a flower child, a love goddess, innocently and enthusiastically in love with love and everything that just comes naturally. A lamb that has strayed among wolves, thinking them sheep.

Pope and the Professor had made no plans as to how they would approach the Love-in Girl if they found her. They had no special reason to think they would catch up with her at a cabin party. Nevertheless Pope's mind is racing in a direction parallel to the Professor's. The party has shifted into high gear with her appearance, and the room is hazy with smoke and thick with the babble of voices, all the guys revving up their engines.

Pope's voice breaks easily through the din, establishing a stunned silence.

"Brothers and honorary sisters," he starts. Everyone turns to look at him. He has stepped forward and stands with his thumbs hooked into the pockets of his jeans, elbows out. He is drunk, but the only evidence of his condition is that he is in the process of delivering a formal address. "As you all know, a friendly young lady has hit town"—he beams at her, and she gazes at him wide-eyed—"who seems to inscribe to a lot of the articles of faith we all do too, and anybody can see she fits right in. But Dillingham ain't part of California . . ." He pauses, to let that fact sink in or to recall what it was he was about to say, ". . . and not everyone in these parts is civilized enough to know how to treat a young lady like her." He has assumed his serious and sincere look, an expression so open and innocent as to appear sheepish. "So I think it's only right and proper for D Inn Crowd to take her under our wing and kind of . . . look after her." He pauses again, a long pause for effect, while his audience stares at him. Then he thrusts out his chin and cranks up his voice another couple of decibels, so that the coda of his address comes across with the authority and volume of a bullhorn. *"I move we make her an honorary tundra bunny right here and now!"*

A moment of dazed silence follows, probably not so much to let the idea sink in as to recover from the impact of its delivery. Then the room bursts into cheers and whistles.

Well, that's okay, thinks the Professor, I can follow that lead and turn it to my advantage.

He is about as drunk as Pope, and about as high and open in all directions. Anything goes when the whistle blows.

The Love-in Girl, who by all appearances has been transfixed by Pope and his speech, partly no doubt because of the power of attention bestowed on her by whichever of the psychedelics she is on, and partly because she has never been exposed to people like this or their parochial terminology, now screams in delighted disbelief: *"Tundra bunny! Oh, wow!"*

Her escort, however, glancing around at this crew of wild and drunken fishermen into whose midst his own schemes for the Love-in Girl have betrayed him, looks extremely uneasy. His face is fixed in a broad smile, to be sure, but his eyes are darting hither and thither like a pair of trapped mice.

"Hold on there just a minute," another not-quite-so-voluminous voice interrupts. Kenny gets up from the big couch and swaggers to the middle of the room, eyebrows at thirty-five-degree angles. He is a big man around Dillingham, one of the Brandon boys, highliners all, and he has decided to quarterback this play (extricating himself from Dark Dolly in the process). "Brother Pope"—he turns Robert Mitchum eyes on his grinning pal—"I'm afraid you're forgetting something. Before we can induct this here fine lady into our order . . . don't we need a *quorum?*"

Most of the people present haven't the bleariest idea of what a quorum might be. Some think Kenny might mean a quarantine: After all, she's from Outside. Kenny's eyes rove coolly over the puzzled faces like Terry Bradshaw reading the defense. When his eyes fall on the Love-in Girl, who is watching him with big brown orbs of curiosity, his eyebrows go to forty-five degrees and he throws his pass. "Gotta keep these Indians in single file, y'know," he explains confidentially. "Of course all the brothers want you—you know, as a honorary member. But we gotta follow proper procedures and all, or it won't stick. And so forth and so on. E pluribus unum, habeas corpus, that sort of thing."

But the Professor's mind is covered with the stickum of craftiness, and like some alert and cunning linebacker he is onto the play and cops an interception.

"Brother Brandon," he says quietly, slipping into the subdued space behind Kenny's challenge while leaning against the kitchen doorjamb, "in the present instance I believe you'll find, if you consult the rules of order, that we don't need a quorum." All eyes are on him now, including Love-in's big browns. "Because you see, a priori and ex post facto and most especially de facto, we *are* a quorum!" He has no clearer idea of what that can mean than do the rest of them, but it sounds legitimate. The Professor, after all, is a real professor and, moreover, holds the title Secretary of D Inn Crowd.

Louder cheers and whistles. Dark Dolly reaches out and pulls Kenny down next to her.

"You tell 'em, Prop," Danny Johanson shouts. "We want the Love-in Girl!" (Danny is one of D Inn Crowd's Board of Directors who, for reasons of his own, always refers to the Professor as Prop.)

That young lady's mouth drops open. This is the first time she has heard her title. "Love-in Girl!?" She looks from Danny to the Professor, whom she hadn't noticed before. The Professor's eyes twinkle into hers, she sees with some confusion, as though he knows her—not necessarily personally.

"Okay, the ayes have it," the Professor concludes with a private pun and abrogating due process. "Now," he continues, thinking on his feet, "as your secretary I do believe it's my duty, as per our bylaws op cit *de gustibus non est disputandum*, to take the young lady aside and explain in more detail and clear manifestation what our noble brotherhood and honorary sisterhood are all about."

Suiting the action to the words, he strides across the room without a wobble and takes her by the hand, she faintly smiling and wide-eyed (ah—and more to the point—wide-pupiled: Still, thinks the Professor, in the land where love and freedom live in conjugal bliss . . . ). He turns officiously to the group, who have followed the general drift of the proceedings with no little glee. "We'll return when I feel her understanding is firm."

More shouts and whistles and some girlish giggles. The Fish and Game guy remains frozen in place, and Kenny sits there wondering what happened to his play.

The Professor leads her into the little bedroom, where there is just room enough for the two of them to stand between the foot of the bed and the mirrored dresser and where in the mirror his eyes fall upon the Tiger on the bed, whom he recognizes at once, a notorious Tiger, almost as horrific in sleep as awake.

Oh, shit! thinks the Professor. I didn't know about *him*.

But love conquers all. With one eye on the mirror and the other on the sweet thing he has by the hand, he begins, trusting that the muse of spontaneity, being close kin to John Barleycorn, will provide the right words in the right order at the right time, thus clearing the way for right action. Barleycorn's inspiration, however, isn't really verbal at all. What fills the Professor's sails is not the wind of verbiage but the pneuma of desire. He sees that the rim of color around her hugely black pupils is golden brown, that delicate wisps of hair curl along her neck, and that her lips are definitely not those of a man, nor is the slender softness of her hand lightly clasping his. Then too, his body, with a will of its own, is responding to her proximity as the north end of one magnet would respond to juxtaposition with the south end of another. It's true that the Professor's mouth is uttering words, whole sentences running together nonstop, but as the medium is the message, his eyes and hands are what communicate, both hands now around her small but palpable waist and drawing her in, his eyes dropping to her mouth and his head following like a tethered donkey, when the beast on the bed stirs, growls, and thrashes about as though struggling back up to its own form of demiconsciousness, becoming aware that intruders have entered its den.

Because the instinct for survival (fight or flight, in this case clearly the latter) is almost as strong as love, the Professor swings around and in so doing releases the girl, who with kaleidoscope eyes sees both the menace on the bed rearing up and the drop-jawed expression of her tutor and decides to let Fish and Game save her. She exits swiftly.

The Tiger fixes its demiconsciousness upon the figure standing there with its mouth open and says, "Hey, you—"

"Yeah, okay," the Professor says. He speaks reassuringly as to a small child, and with a big smile. "Sure. You probably could use a hair of the dog. I'll go tell everyone you're awake." He doesn't wait for a response.

Pope meets him at the door. "What the fuck did you say to her?"

"Why? What?" The Professor is pushing his friend away from the bedroom door and toward the front door, ignoring the confused looks and questions coming his way from the others.

"She's gone out of here like—"

"Never mind that. Come on." He grabs Pope by the arm. "I'll explain in a minute." And over his shoulder as he closes the door behind them: "Go get 'em, Tiger."

❋

By now it is full light sometime early in the morning. The air smells good coming in off the bay, the clean salt air of the sea and the distant cries of the gulls. Pope and the Professor are still drunk and suddenly very hungry. As the Professor is telling Pope what happened in the bedroom, they turn as with one mind down the empty gravel road that leads to the small-boat harbor and the good ship *Diane*, where the food is.

Pope goes below to see what his appetite can find while the Professor sits down on the captain's stool on deck. He gazes off astern at the silver-and-gold flashing of the saw grass in the wind, a flamenco dancer in gypsy clothes and bracelets and earrings glinting. He wishes he had seen her dancing at the Sea Inn to the McKenzie song that always makes him nostalgic for Syracuse and the hippie scene. In his mind's eye he can picture her, the lithe female form undulating, hair tossing as she dips and turns, long brown-and-golden hair tossing.

Then he seems to hear voices, the bar crowd responding, *Ole! Ole!*, voices whirled away with the wind outside his head, and then suddenly loud and clear when the wind dies: "It's tequila time!" and lo and behold here comes the Chaplain out of the grass waving a jug of tequila time and Freeman behind him with another jug but without a shirt and next to him Danny Johanson banging the back of a guitar like a drum. Danny catches the Professor's eye and raises the guitar aloft. "Hey, hey, look what we got. Where's Pope? Come on, Prop, this party's just getting started. We need some music!" He starts singing "Ruby, Ruby," sliding down the cutbank, with Kenny right behind him, minus Dark Dolly or any visible wounds, and there she is again! The Love-in Girl, like Venus rising from the sea of grass, attended by the pretty native girl who had been making eyes at Freeman. Love-in's bearded rescuer is nowhere in evidence. Maybe the Tiger got him.

Pope hears them and pops up on deck, guitar in hand, laughing. Their appearance is like a papal decree. He thrusts out his hand for the tequila, which the Chaplain administers. Freeman hands the other jug to the Professor. Everyone watches approvingly as Pope and the Professor tilt their heads back and take a couple of good long belts.

So, with the brethren and sistren all over the *Diane*, it is now a boat party. Pope and the Professor sit on the starboard gunwale with the two guitars and bang out "Proud Mary," singing loud and with gusto. Kenny and Louie sit opposite them clapping time and coming in on the chorus. Freeman has cornered his pretty girl belowdecks, and Danny and the Chaplain are in the stern dancing with a couple of bunnies who have appeared out of nowhere and are unknown to the Professor. The sun is high and intense enough now to boil the tequila in their veins, and it's tequila time between every number, like throwing gas on a fire. The Love-in Girl has been swept right into this vortex where the old god Dionysus still rules. She is up and dancing in half time, as though in answer to the Professor's unspoken asking, her arms raised, her eyes almost closed, now and again tossing her long brown golden hair in response to the beat. The man's shirt she wears is loose as a tunic, and her neat little unconstrained breasts lift and press against the cotton as she moves.

❋

There are thresholds in the chemistry of consciousness, borderlines between everyday reality and . . . others. Various substances are passports across those borders. And different ones admit you into different countries. For the Love-in Girl, already predisposed by her hippie head space, it is the tequila at the tail end of her acid trip that sweeps her across to the other side. For the Professor, whose body with bright eyes is rising and who is partially aware of but wholly unconcerned about the fact that he is removing his shirt, it is Bristol Bay itself plus the tequila that greases the palm of the immigration officer and zonks the border guards, propelling him into the land of Right Now, where not only is there no tomorrow but there is not even time in a minute: If you want to do it, you will do it right now. Since what the Professor wants to do is dance with the lovelier and lovelier Love-in Girl, he is right in front of her and right in step with her to the beat of the music. The semaphores of his eyes flash through her half-closed lids with the message that this is just all

right. When he finishes taking off his shirt—whistling, stomp-
ing, clapping, Johanson's "Show us how to do it, Prop!" and
Pope's big voice the medium in which they dance—she is with
him and smiling and taking off hers.

The Professor isn't horny, he is high, and it is just all right
that they take their shirts off in the white eye of the madcap
sun. He doesn't lust for her. Lust means wanting, it lives in time.
The Professor lives in right now, which has enough. He has all
of her he wants right now. The whoops and hollers, stomps and
whistles—everyone has gathered around them—seem somehow
muted, at a distance, a background drone. She fills his horizon.
They are sweating, everyone is sweating, their bodies glistening.

"Hey, Man," she smiles at him in an easy way, looking up
at him with bent head, "you got a cold beer or something?"

Still in step with her, he leans forward and kisses her lightly
on the lips (a miracle of yielding softness).

"You got it, sweetheart," he says.

And still dancing, he turns and hops up onto the gunwale
to step across to Kenny's boat, where he knows the beer is, and
the thought strikes him that he is hungry, and he wonders if he
really intends to raid Kenny's larder at this time, with the Love-
in Girl dancing topless behind him, but he figures the question
will take care of itself when he gets there (you don't make plans
when you live in right now). But it happens that some power
greater or wiser than his willingness to go on partying takes
command of the situation and simply and abruptly calls it quits.
Blake said you never know what is enough until you know what
is too much. Well then, too much, Professor. Lights out, right
here and right now. As luck would have it, right here and right
now is midstride between the two boats. Gravity is ready. The
Professor goes down into the gray mud, its pleasant silky coolness
his last sensation. And his last thought, "Well, okay, fuck
it." So they have to haul him up out of the mud, he being
altogether unaware, totally sublime, given over to sweet oblivion. They wash him off with wet towels, his reckless, swaggering,

tough-guy pals, grinning because he has gotten drunk and crazy and passed out and because in so doing he has told them he is just like them—peccable, maculate, vulnerable, foolish, going all the way, till the wheels fall off and burn.

*I'm in with D Inn Crowd*
*I go where D Inn Crowd goes*

They slip him into a sleeping bag there on deck. Pope goes below and comes back up with a cup of flour. They stand around the Professor's inert form intoning a kind of dirge in pidgin Latin while Pope sprinkles a little flour over the dear departed brother. Then they carry him below out of the sun.

❁

I awoke some time a day or so later in my bunk. I was alone. It was sunny again, the wind still whipping through the saw grass outside the porthole. The *Diane* was afloat, water patterns glinting on the ceiling. The Love-in Girl was gone. A fishing period was set for 4:00 A.M. the next day. We would leave on the ebb about 1:00 A.M.

❁

From the moral perspective, what can be said in defense of the Professor's behavior? In Mrs. Grundy's opinion, not much. But Mrs. Grundy is a stock response sloshing around in the stinking backwaters of the slough of judgmental absolutes. In the relative universe of real people we find the Professor off the reservation, running with an outlaw crowd, traveling the road of excess, striking out for the hinterlands of civilization: "where the lawmen can't find you and the wild wolves don't care what you did when you were living in that other world back there" (from one of Steve's songs). That he should, with the complicity of occasion, get loaded and break loose from Mrs. Grundy's compound and count a little coup on the girls is no more than natural. Men and women, in truth, everywhere and in all times have used psychotropic substances and indulged in dalliance. The rest is rhetoric. This is a work of nonfiction, not Disneyland.

# 8

# FIASCO, OR WHAT BECAME OF

# *PORT N STORM*

Pope and I were hustling again, late on the tide and late starting for the Naknek side. Most of the fish were supposed to return to the Naknek/Kvichak watershed in 1969. It was not expected to be a good year. "Most" would not be many. Forecasts and fishermen were both down in the mouth. So getting in on every open period was important. Any missed period would come back to haunt us the following winter. I was no longer a salaried professor sure of his next meal. I had moved with my family the autumn before to the Iliamna Lake wilderness near Pope: re-signed my professorship, sold the farm, and went for broke. If we didn't do at least pretty good fishing that summer, broke is what I'd get. Next winter would be showing its ribs.

We were scheduled to be lowered into the water on this tide, what was left of it. At best we could catch the tail end of the ebb and have to buck tide the last hour or so down the Nush-agak. There had been some problems and delays with a couple of the boats ahead of us, and very little water remained around the end of the dock where the launching boom was. Boats tied off the pilings a little ways up the dock were already high and dry. I was tense inside, though I tried not to let it show: "Above all, don't panic" was the fisherman's mantra.

We walked along behind the *Diane*, which sat on dollies

being towed to the launching rig. The last boat in line before us was in the slings and being lowered, its crew standing on board. I sensed or heard something close behind and looked back. Roy, the port engineer, sat at the wheel of one of those powerful little cars that buzz around docks and warehouses. He was watching me with pale blue eyes and a Mona Lisa smile, and looming up behind him like his pet shark was the sharp green nose of *Port N Storm,* with all eight of Pope's fifty-five gallon drums piled in the stern.

Uh-oh, what's this? A sudden bad feeling turned my stomach over. I grabbed Pope by the arm. "Hey Gene, what the fuck's this all about?" My voice was louder than it was supposed to be ("Above all, don't panic"). Pope swung around and saw Roy grinning and *Port N Storm* looming. He went tight-lipped and dropped back alongside Roy, who sat there like a stone Buddha.

"Shit, Roy—you're not putting the Professor's boat in too—?"

"Yep," Roy replied in his Texas drawl, "sure am. Right on top of the *Diane.*" His eyes twinkled like icicles in the afternoon sun. He and his crew of mechanics worked on boats but never went to sea. Their work was safe and not exciting; in fact it was boring, with long hours. So they enjoyed the trials, tribulations, and fuckups of the fishermen, especially the harum-scarum fishermen like Pope and the Professor.

We protested vigorously, in colorful language. Fuck! We couldn't possibly handle both boats now. Shit! There was barely enough fucking water to get away from the fucking dock with just the fucking *Diane.* Goddammit! Even if we managed by some miracle to take care of *Port N Storm* too, we'd have to buck tide all the way down the fucking Nushagak. Jesus Christ! This was the wrong occasion to be returning the boat to its rightful owner. There just wasn't *time.* All of which tickled Roy and prompted the thin line of his mouth to imitate a little smile.

"No use you boys telling me sad stories," he said. "I'm only doing what I been told. Better go cry on Jack's shoulder. Maybe he'll feel your pain." (Jack was the cannery superintendent and could never be located. He was always much too busy to be found.)

The reason for this unannounced and unexpected procedure was not far to seek. *Port N Storm* had been parked at the cannery—in an out-of-the-way spot but nevertheless on cannery property—for too long. With Pope and me on hand for the *Diane*'s launching, the cannery boss had seen his chance to clear the decks of a boat that wasn't going to be fishing for him anyway. That it would cause us serious dismay was not his concern. He was the boss and did what was best for the company: fishermen weren't the company.

There was no time left for further protestations. The *Diane* was in the slings and suspended over the edge of the dock. Pope and I jumped on board and rode her down to the water. We slid the slings out from under as fast as we could. Pope darted to the wheel, started her up, and pulled away from the dock. When I looked up, *Port N Storm*'s green bottom was descending on us like the final curtain.

The mud was showing now, only a dozen or so feet away. There was barely enough water left to float us. Maybe what Muhammad said is true—that paradise is under the shadow of the sword—but I doubt that anyone believes it when the shadow falls. As *Port N Storm* settled into the water, Pope brought the *Diane* alongside, and while I worked the slings out from under her he tied up. There were no options. We had to try to drag *Port N Storm* into the small-boat harbor and hopefully slide back out on what would by then be little more than mud. We had earlier appropriated *Port N Storm*'s starter battery for the *Diane*, so she couldn't move under her own power.

We were only a minute or two away from the dock when Pope started swearing. "What the *fuck* is that boat made out of? I'm full bore right now and we're barely moving. Feels like we're towing the whole fucking dock." He stood tiptoe to see down to *Port N Storm*'s waterline. "Shit! Is she taking on water?"

With those words an image projected itself onto the screen of my mind. In great clarity of detail I saw the two drain plugs, black rubber and brass with levers to lock them in place, lying in the bilge of my boat under the afterdeck, each one precisely next to the drain hole it was designed to seal watertight when installed. I had taken them out myself after the previous season to drain and air the hull, which was proper procedure. Then Pope had "temporarily" stored the drums on board. Then we had been taken by surprise by the cannery's sudden move in launching the boat. And now *Port N Storm* was filling with water because the drain plugs were not in place.

I leaped across and yes, I could see water down among the drums, above the floorboards. The *Diane* was beginning to list with the increasing weight tied alongside. I started wrestling with the drums as one struggles in a nightmare, with desperate effort and to no effect. They were heavy and some were wedged in tight. They would have to be cleared from the afterdeck before I could lift the floorboards and feel for the plugs in the bilge. It was too much to carry each drum up forward and find a place for it. I was in slow motion, and everything else was fast forward. There wouldn't be room anyway, so I started heaving them over the side. They made big splashes. Maybe the gang up on the dock thought we were after a submarine. Several drums still blocked my way as we entered the channel to the small-boat harbor. Where the channel opened into the harbor basin, Pope yelled over, "We gotta cut her loose right here. Can't drag her any further, and we're running out of water. Throw the hook out toward shore as far as you can."

We didn't want *Port N Storm* to drift around with the tides half submerged in the channel, and maybe if the anchor held we could salvage the boat at some later low water. By now the adrenaline was racing through my body like Popeye's spinach. I skipped up to the bow, grabbed the anchor, and heaved. Our anchors were attached to a heavy chain, which in turn was supposed to be attached to the bowline, which was supposed to be attached to the bow cleat. The anchor and chain went sailing out like a kite with a tail. They arced through the air for what was truly an amazing distance, almost reaching the shore. The end of the chain however wasn't attached to the bowline, which lay coiled at my feet like a sleeping cat.

"Jesus Christ!" Pope roared.

I stood there watching the anchor and chain disappear into destiny.

"Fuck it!" he shouted. "Let's go!"

I turned and performed an Olympic broad jump to land on the *Diane* as he swung her about, or more exactly *slid* her about, in the mud. Our churning propeller dug its own channel until we caught up with the tide and headed wide open down Nushagak Bay.

❀

*Port N Storm* died in the small-boat harbor. She was dragged about by the tides, and boats had to dodge her half-submerged body. Then finally a tender hit her and sent her down for good. At the end of the season, after we returned from Naknek, a local fellow I didn't know, one of the Seventh Day Adventists, offered me a few bucks for her remains as is, where is. I accepted the money, glad to be freed of the responsibility, and used it to buy a couple of commemorative rounds at the Sea Inn Bar.

Fishermen are tough guys, and tough guys don't weep. But the tough guys downing the commemorative drinks with me knew how I felt, way back in there. Our boats are with us through thick and thin, and we get to know every inch of them, very much as a man with his good woman. Under our surface regard of brass-tacks utility, we loved our boats.

So farewell to the good ship *Port N Storm*. She had had a rich and varied life, as they say, full of adventures, hardships, and triumphs. And that was true. She had been my first boat, and we had shared some memorable times. I was very sorry to lose her, especially like that. I had wanted to take her back to the lake after the season, retire her to her proper element, but it was not her fate to live out her days as a genteel lady on the fresh, clear waters of Iliamna Lake.

# 9

# A  NIGHT  ON  THE  OUTSIDE

The word came suddenly in the season of '70: Fish and Game had extended the outer limits. We could move out, go to the fish, since the fish hadn't come to us.

The fleet was anchored in the Naknek River, waiting. The run was overdue, but it was coming. The advance guard of a gigantic school of salmon, the biggest in years, had been sighted from the air off Port Heiden. That was way down the Alaska Peninsula, way past the original outer-limit markers, past Egegik, down where the water was blue and deep, where the water was ocean.

We had been idle, the nets neatly coiled in the stern, the boat gassed up, stocked with grub, water, and fuel oil for cooking and heat. Waiting for the fish. *The fish!* For some of these fishermen it was still the fish that counted, that meant more than the dollar, though it meant that too, no getting around it. One night someone had scrawled in big Magic Marker letters on the graffiti wall of the Sea Inn Bar's toilet: "The Fish!" Just that. "The Fish!" I saw it above my head as I stood, no doubt as unsteadily as the writer must have, at the urinal. Amid all the voices, jukebox noise, and macho tensions of the drunken bar, someone, most likely a native from one of the villages, had thought of the fish, the rudimentary fact of the fish, and as I stood there looking at the scrawled words I saw them—the fish—in my mind's eye, the salmon close-packed, moving through the silent waters, single-minded to spawn and die. And the men and the women, anciently as now, were waiting for them to come into their nets. It was still the fish the villagers thought of—the great gift of the salmon, which they would smoke cool and long to last the winter, the fillets turning dark red, seared and dry, with a taste you got to like. That was more than the money, the flesh and blood fish more than the symbol.

Even the scratch fishing had hardly been worth it for most of us, almost nothing showing, so we were mainly just waiting, and waiting meant mainly hanging out in the bars: clumping down the muddy streets of Naknek—to what? There were only the bars. One was the kind of bloody honky-tonk joint typical of Bristol Bay—linoleum booths and vinyl tables—where you would be guaranteed a fight merely by staying late enough into the night. The other, however, was a miracle of rare device, for Bristol Bay. It was owned and operated by a past-middle-age lady of refined sensibilities, another Alaskan ex-dancer who had set herself up in business on the proceeds of her younger and fleshier days. At one time she had surely been a looker and, most likely, in Alaska then, when women, no less lookers, were scarce to nonexistent, a man-killer: Power corrupts, and in her time and place she would have been a pearl of great price and therefore a femme fatale.

The bar sat alone on the edge of the bluff above the river. A spur of the town's one gravel road went to it, little more than a pathway, with planks across the bigger puddles. It sat amid saw grass waving in the wind under the big sky. It was a low-slung log building, and very old, weathered gray, but with a startling border of carefully tended wildflowers—small delicate blooms of blue and lavender, red and purple, white and yellow— that stood out brilliantly against the dark gray logs. Inside was another world, a place apart, what Hemingway would have rec-ognized as a clean, well-lighted place: dark massive ridge pole and purlins with fishnets looped across the ceiling, with clusters of the old glass-and-twine Japanese buoys hanging here and there reflecting the green-and-red lights of antique ship's lanterns scattered about, heavy oak tables and captain's chairs, a large beveled mirror behind the bar creating illusions of depth and spatters of colored lights.

The lady's specialty was exotic and very expensive drinks. Her clientele, in black hip boots annealed with fish scales and smelling of fish and engine oil, who normally drank whatever happened to be available straight from the bottle, no quarter given or taken, hovered over their pink and orange apparitions like high school sophomores at the corner ice cream parlor. Roughshod as they were, uncouth as they might be deemed, they enjoyed the poetry of the place, this improbable taste of something fine.

Pope and I, Kenny, Louie, Danny, and Bill Miner (a fisherman and friend, though not one of D Inn Crowd) were thus comfortably engaged, about two drinks to euphoria, feeling warm inside and out. Mellow. Our legs were well stretched out, and we regarded our hostess in kindly fashion, the little lady with wispy red-blond hair dyed too many times, hair reinforced now with concrete sprays, the lady with thin arms, thick waist, and layers of sourdough pancake makeup (which almost worked in the half-light), imagining her twenty or thirty years ago, a blond bombshell, a man-killer you'd be willing to be killed for, each of us coming increasingly to believe that at any moment a bevy of coed cannery workers was about to appear, blondes, brunettes, and redheads, shyly or boldly questing for the company of rugged and romantic fishermen, when suddenly a big hard-edged voice freighted with the self-assurance of an emissary from the real world of dollars and sense announced summarily that the fishing was now open all the way down. Whoever it was said it once, standing backlighted in the doorway, then turned and departed without so much as an apology.

A cryptic message, yes. But enough said.

Certainly we were all laid back and cozy, sliding into a glass onion. Too bad. Fun may be fun, but business is business. We were Americans, and in America the golden rule is: Business before pleasure. Take care of business and the pleasure will take care of itself. (Which doesn't seem to work that way actually, because by the time you get done taking care of business you don't have much left in you for fun, even if you think you could use some. You've lost the skill.)

In any case options were limited or nonexistent. The fishing season was short, the winters long and potentially hungry. Common sense under these circumstances found that rich ugly old maid Prudence more attractive than the ex-dancer or the bevy of coeds (all the more so since the coeds weren't there).

We looked at one another, seeking a little manly willpower.

"Fuck!" said Pope, who had none.

He was fishing an open skiff that year, by choice. He didn't like the responsibilities and upkeep demands attached to ownership of a regulation gillnetter and had sold me the *Diane* at the close of the previous season. But he also didn't like the prospect of fishing his mangy skiff on really big water where he couldn't make a dash for port if need be. He especially didn't like seeing a budding party abruptly clipped.

"I second that," Louie frowned, looking dour.

Kenny glanced at his partner with lazy eyelids and said nothing. The Brandons were highliners, fishermen to the core. Kenny Brandon didn't suffer future shock in this situation. He was after the fish—here, there, or anywhere else. He was as at home in a boat on the water as a weevil in a boll of cotton. Couldn't be nicer.

"Shit!" said Danny, with an expression that reminded me he had done time for assault and battery. "I gotta find Chucky. If we're going down Pilot Point way, I'll need him. He can work the pump while I steer." (It took cooperation as well as courage to maintain his boat's superior standing to the sea.)

Bill Miner laughed in his easy, whiskery way. He was the

kind of easygoing unself-conscious man who faced all kinds of weather and never saw himself, only the weather. (And yet, while writing this book, I heard Bill was in jail for killing a man.)

As for me, stepping out of the warmth into the cold wind driving in off the bay, I felt like a man sizing up his prospects while walking the last mile. The wind was not only cold but hard, my moral fiber not only warm but soft. The thought of the loveless dock stilted over the mud, the mindless water lapping, nudging the boats, the oil and gas smells, the feel of the wet lines . . . and the question behind it all: Were we seaworthy? Could the *Diane,* with a thrown rod knocking against the block, make it there and back? Drizzle on the embers of my mood.

When Gregory Peck or Jimmy Stewart did this kind of scene, it always seemed sort of heroic, a stiff-upper-lip sort of thing, with maybe a touch of gallows humor thrown in, quipping in the face of danger or hardship. I always assumed that was how I'd do it too, but actually I felt neither heroic nor humorous. As I dragged myself down to the dock, words ran through my head, a madcap jig juxtaposing images from diverse and incongruous worlds: Are there happy days after high school when bilge pumps decide not to work and the sea can't tell the difference between a happy ending and drowning? Better pack away your creased white captain's uniform, because the fish slime on this love boat stains dark red. Does six-ply nylon love the red gills of silvery salmon that it grasps them so tightly? And do the round impersonal eyes of dying fish regard the fisherman with understanding and love, as the cut worm is said to forgive the plow? Is this trip necessary?

For my son Steve and me (Steve was my partner that year) this trip should not have been necessary or even plausible: the thrown rod knocking, the untrustworthy bilge pump, the unreliable ignition. Wherever we went, we went slowly, in deference to the thrown rod (a burst of speed could shoot it through the block). So if we needed a surge of power, we wouldn't get it, and if we took on water, the pump might or might not be willing to belch it back. Sometimes in fishing it's necessary that certain things be done quickly: Your end buoy way out there suddenly gets caught in a tide rip, say, and is being pulled toward another boat's outside shackle. You need to start your engine right away and drag your nets clear. The *Diane*, however, might or might not respond to normal starting procedures. Pushing the starter button might or might not initiate the series of contained explosions desired. Pouring gasoline down the carburetor's open throat might or might not stimulate a heartbeat of power. Hooking our spare battery in series with the one that was supposed to be self-sufficient often worked. Apparently the double electrical whammy, a kind of shock therapy, rescrambled the circuits—goosing a condenser, perhaps, or installing stamina into a weak resistor—and the Chrysler would spring into ostensible well-being. The side effects of this galvanic treatment, however, could prove more dire than the original malady. It could—and eventually would—burn out the starter coils. And that would be that.

These considerations did not foster confidence. *Con-fidence*: "with faith, to go with faith." If we went, it would have to be with faith, because reason would have abandoned ship. Faith not in the boat (such faith would have been misplaced) but in— what? In nothing reasonable, certainly, in nothing palpable, measurable, or scientific. Blind faith, then. Absurd faith (I believe *because* it is absurd). As Gene Pope proceeded by dead reckoning, we moved out in blind faith. A lot of things could happen, a lot of things could go wrong; and conventional wisdom advises that whatever can go wrong will go wrong. And if something did go wrong, we would have only ourselves to look to for the help we were ill-equipped to provide. But while reason might be right, he had no balls. And he hadn't signed on anyway. So we went with faith, and a little spirit: See what happens.

Not that I was altogether foolhardy and hadn't even tried to get the *Diane* shipshape. I had submitted a work order more than a week before, but the port engineer was backed up and never got to us. The bona fide highliners came first. Nor could we find a substitute engine. We would have to pamper the old Chrysler and hope for the best. Nevertheless the fish were out there. By the end of this period we could be two thousand dollars further away from hungry. I had a family to feed from the proceeds now, further inspiring my willingness to take risks. All the other guys had headed out too, even Pope. After all, that's what we were there for. To fish. Circumstances for Steve and me were not propitious, granted, but then circumstances seldom are. "Adventure!" Pope said. Were we perfectly prepared, it might be only a job. We were going for it. And as for drowning, well, to repeat a favorite mantra, as Shakespeare wrote somewhere, we owe God a death, and he who pays today is quits for tomorrow, albeit I was easier applying this philosophy to myself than to Steve. Years before, when Steve was a boy, I had dreamed one night he was drowning and I couldn't reach him. It was a nightmare I never forgot. The awful feeling came back whenever the image rose in my mind of him under water looking toward me with wide, terrified eyes. It haunted me with misgivings about his fishing there in the dangerous waters of Bristol Bay, and now the dread feeling returned in face of this dubious venture into big and unknown seas with him on board the ailing *Diane*. But what then? Was I to leave him ashore with his mother, surround him with concern, muffle him away from the strong winds of life? That would be a worse kind of drowning. He was carefree, bold in spirit, and I remembered how he looked back in '65 standing with Pope watching our nets go up in smoke, the life exuberant in him, his face ruddy, his blue eyes blazing, and the wind blowing through his hair. No way I would let my fears for him squelch that. Even love has its limits and must let go.

❁

At first there were other boats around us heading out through the chop. We followed known channels down past Johnson Hill.

But as the bay opened into ocean, the boats meandered apart. Soon it was just a little toy boat here and there in the distance, disappearing among the waves. Whatever comfort or guidance they represented was fast fading, along with the light.

So we were heading down and out, very possibly in more ways than one. The short chop of the shallower reaches of Kvichak Bay were maturing into waves of deep-sea caliber, waves a thirty-two-foot fish boat has to climb up and slide down, and the water had changed from dirty yellow to clear blue-black. The strip of land off our port side got farther and farther away, and there was just me, my son Steve, the ailing *Diane*, and the friendly ocean. Water loves to float your boat or, with equal mind, sink it. Makes no difference to the water. It doesn't mean to be mean, but fact is it can be hostile to our biology. In its fresh and unadulterated state it is excellent, and necessary, to drink, but in any state deadly to inhale. When warm enough, it's a perfect medium in which to bathe or play, but if cold enough long enough (in Bristol Bay, about three to five minutes) it becomes inimical to human life-support systems. Hypothermia or drowning, whichever comes first.

Steve knew all this as well as I did, but as far as I could tell the only thing on his mind was the adventure of it—a feature perhaps of his youth, but also of his personal spirit, a lifelong gift to him from the great unknown. I had long ago determined not to damp that spirit with cautions and fears about safety, and I was struggling now to bolster that determination. Yes, I told myself again, better a spirit ready for life or death than a long existence of nervous insecurity. I was glad he was with me. It was the right way to go.

My immediate concern, however, was where, in all that trackless expanse of water, we should lay out our nets. Surely the fish weren't just everywhere. Where might we expect to find them? Back up in the bay they were funneled into relatively narrow confines, but out here there were no channels or bars, no bit of water more likely than another. I decided our best bet would be to lay out a test shackle, listen in on the radio, and see what happened. If no fish hit and we heard nothing over the radio, we would pull in and run down a ways farther and try again, and so on into the night.

The evening sun was low to the water, obscured by clouds, the wind steady out of the southwest, cresting the waves lightly at about twelve feet. Steve and I stood together at the wheel looking out along the corkline for hits or maybe a jumper— some sign that there were at least a few fish in the area. With the engine silent, the only sounds were the hush of the wind and the hiss of the cresting waves rolling by.

As we watched, a broad ray of the low sun broke through the clouds, and waves that had been darkly opaque a moment ago were suddenly as though lit up from within. They looked like liquid sapphire. And in every luminous wave we saw clearly the darting bullet shapes of strings of salmon. It was as though a light switch had been thrown in a dark cave to reveal to modern eyes the dazzling artwork of ancient ancestors. Every-thing was aglow, the clouds on fire, the undulating corkline ir-idescent with foam, the waves like fabulous gems held up to the light, even the workaday *Diane* burnished in gold. The fish were everywhere, constant streams of them streaking through the wa-ter. We stood stunned by the sight. We had never seen or heard of anything like this. This was like Moses before the burning bush, a kind of revelation.

I turned to Steve to say something. "But look!" he cried, his arm shooting out, pointing. "They're dodging the net!"

It was true. We could see them heading right for the net, then diving under it or turning sharply and streaking along its length and around or under the boat. In the silty water of the upper bay the net would be invisible, but out here the fish could see the webbing. As a result, although the water was alive with fish, we caught relatively few of them. But we didn't care about that. We were seeing something whose worth couldn't be calculated in the currency of commerce. When Moses stood before the burning bush he wasn't counting quail.

It lasted for less than a minute, a spot of time. Then, like a curtain closing or a god withdrawing, the clouds drew across the sun, and the fish disappeared inside the everyday waves. But I knew that what we had seen was the reality of the sea and the fish, the numinous world habitually closed to us by single vision and Newton's sleep.

Clouds spread across the sky, and the wind began to pick up. A chill filtered into my bones. I stood on deck looking around, very much aware that this little arc of wood rising and falling with the waves was our only security in face of what now felt like the cold indifference of the sea. The low silhouette of the coastline off our port side was barely visible and offered no comfort. There were no lights of a town or road, no harbor lights. The land was barren and unknown to me. Even if there had been some natural cove or protective headland over there, should things get really rough, I would never be able to find it in the dark. I imagined the surf breaking white along the rocks or against the bluffs. We had best stay well offshore, in deep water, keep watch, and ride it out until daylight. I turned in a slow circle, looking. Not a mast light anywhere, no red and green lights of a boat under way. The radio was silent. We had this stretch of ocean to ourselves. Or more likely it was the other way around.

It started raining, sky and sea fused into a darkness, only the whitecaps showing dim, driving past, the corkline quickly disappearing astern. We got into our rain gear and pulled the net in, picking the fish as they came over the roller, and then ran the shackle back out to act as a sea anchor, keeping our stern into the waves. If it got much rougher, we would switch ends so that the pointed bow faced into the waves instead of the square stern. We might catch some more fish, but that wasn't my main intent. I wanted to hold steady, stern or bow into the waves, without having to use power, which might not be available, and ride out the dark hours. When it got light we would take stock of our situation and decide what next.

There was little likelihood of drifting afoul of another boat—always a liability on a night drift, which was why someone usually stood watch. Certainly this night I wouldn't be catching a little sleep. Not in these waters, with the wind getting stronger. I wanted to be sure some combination of wind and tide didn't push us toward shore. Steve could take a break while I watched, and then when it got light, if everything was okay, maybe I could get a couple of hours' sleep while he stood watch.

We went below, out of the wind and rain, and I turned the oil stove up a notch. The lightbulb was bare and dim but better than nothing. We doffed our rain gear and boots and just sat for a while, soaking up the warmth and the humble but kindly dimensions of the cabin. The boat rose and fell as the waves washed by in a hypnotic rhythm. I could see Steve starting to nod off. No anxiety there. I smiled to myself.

"Well, Sportin' Life," I said, "looks like you're ready for a little shut-eye. So what do you want to dream about?"

"Grandma's cookies," he said, "hot out of the oven." Then he gave me a big smile. "Or Wanda," he added.

The remnant of the boy—Grandma's cookies—and the presence of the young man—Wanda, the beautiful half-native daughter of one of the fishermen I knew a little. I'd seen her and Steve one day earlier in the season sitting together on the bow of her father's boat anchored in the Naknek River, her dark glossy head touching his blond one, and I'd thought, And so the dance goes on.

"Sweet dreams either way," I grinned. "Go ahead, catch forty. I'll give you a shake if anything comes up."

And in a minute he did, right where he was sitting.

I leaned into the radio, hoping to hear one of the guys, maybe saying where he was and what was happening—Kenny or Danny or Pope. There was nothing but buzzing and hissing on the radio. Gene probably didn't even have a radio on his skiff. He was probably out there somewhere hunched over in his doghouse, wet and cold, the rain pelting on the plywood over his head, staring out past his outboards at what he could see of his corkline. I shivered. But Pope was strong and tough and had one big advantage: He knew what he was doing.

I turned the dial from channel to channel but got only more static and buzzing. Maybe no one was on, maybe they were confident enough to be sleeping out the night drift. Or maybe they were way farther down—that far off? No. They couldn't all be that far away. And how in the world did they know where to go? I vowed to myself that in the future I would learn more about fishing and less about partying. I needed to contact someone. Was I out here alone? Had they all pulled in for some reason and run back up, too far off for us to see their lights? Whoa! Remember the code: Above all, don't panic.

I decided to squander a little of the battery to try to raise somebody on the main channel we used.

"The *Wanda B*, the *Wanda B*. The *Diane*. You on, Kenny?"

I waited. Hissing and static. I tried a few more times. Nothing. Even if Kenny and Louie were sleeping, any of the other guys would have answered had they heard. Could be the battery was too low to transmit. Great. And was it too low to crank over the engine when I needed to? I wasn't feeling very good. No more transmissions. But receiving draws very little juice, so I twisted the dial, and this time I heard voices, distant and garbled. I turned up the volume and leaned into the receiver. What came through, scrambled by static, were voices talking, coming in and fading out. But they didn't sound like they were speaking English, and not Eskimo either. Japanese or Russian maybe. I looked out the porthole. No sign of land, no lights anywhere. Nothing but darkness and the dim white crests of the waves. What? Were we rounding the corner, on our way to Japan? Then the weird voices faded and some kind of music came through faintly in the background, music that was weirder than the voices, fading in and out. It was a little like the Beatles' "Number 9" thing—or like something from outer space. The music of the spheres? Or were the voices neither Japanese, Russian, nor native, but Martian? Whoa again. Hold on, Professor.

After all, we were afloat and at the moment warm and dry. Maybe even catching some fish. It was only a few hours till daylight, when at least we could see, clouds or no clouds. No use conjuring up ghosts, getting my bowels in an uproar. Present fears are less than horrible imaginings. Take it one step at a time. Steve's head rested against the hull. Asleep. Good. I got up and pulled on my slicker and went above.

The rain drove in under the pilothouse, icy spikes hitting my face, and I was wide awake. I checked the Fathometer. The luminous green dial assured me we were in plenty of water. Luminous green dials were always a comfort: Yeah, we know what we're doing; we got technology. All right. Plenty of water under us. That was the main thing right now. No bouncing off some kind of hard bottom.

I stared astern for a couple of minutes, blinking from the rain in my eyes. No hits along the few visible fathoms of the net. Okay with me. There would be no survival advantage to having a loaded net to deal with. If the wind picked up more, we would have to switch ends. Right now the stern was dipping fairly sharply into the troughs but riding right back up, no heavy spray coming aboard.

I turned and went below into the warmth and light. Steve was still slumped in the corner, breathing slow and deep. I sat down and in a minute or two found my own head drooping, eyelids wanting to clamp shut. Whoops! Can't have that. There was still some coffee in the pot. I put it on the stove and waited for it to heat up.

Then I heard something, a new sound. It was coming from directly above, a sharp rap, then an interval of silence, then another rap, first to port, then to starboard, then back again. Now what? I looked up, listening. *Tap*, silence, *tap*. From one side to the other. Steve's eyes opened and he sat up, looking at me blankly.

*. . . suddenly there came a tapping,*
*As of someone gently rapping, rapping*
*at my chamber door.*

Poe's poem flashed through my head ridiculously as I sat there and returned Steve's gaze. "Quoth the raven, 'Nevermore.'" Swell. Just the right note for the occasion. I didn't need Poe to spook me. The night and the sea were quite enough. I didn't need any otherworldly ingredients. First the weird voices and weirder music and now this.

"What's that?" Steve asked.

That snapped me to. Yes, indeed, what's that? What in the world (and not out of it) could be making that rapping sound? Certainly no giant raven. It seemed to keep to the rhythm of the waves, like a kind of metronome.

"Better have a look," I said, getting to my feet, once more in the world of cause and effect.

I stepped out on deck and paused, letting my eyes adjust. *Clack.* It came from right behind me, toward the bow. I swung around and saw an arcing movement through the windshield, a dull metallic sheen arcing. The *Diane* not only rose and fell with the waves, it rolled a bit as well, enough to swing the antenna rod, loosed from its upper bracket on the pilothouse, from side to side, slapping down onto the cabin deck, its end hanging out over the water: the radio antenna, tentatively held on board by only its seating in the lower socket flange. Not good. The *Diane* was a cripple. We needed the radio, we might need it badly.

I moved out along the gunwale, holding on to the handrail, to have a closer look. I could make out the socket flange. Only one side was still fastened by a couple of lag bolts, the others apparently pulled out and lost. The bolts still holding could work loose too, and if the antenna went over, the cable to the radio wouldn't be strong enough to keep it from the deep six. I needed to get the flange tightened down with new bolts and replace the upper bracket.

I went below for the hardware and tools I would need. Steve was pulling on his boots. He looked up.

"What is it?" he asked.

"I think we can fix it," I said. "It's the antenna come loose. The bracket's hanging on one screw, and looks like only two bolts in the flange. Maybe you could hold the light for me, shine it through the windshield."

Part of me didn't want him out there—everything above was wet and slippery—but there was no way I was going to tell him to stay below and mind the stove. He wasn't a boy anymore, and he was a good hand. This wasn't a pleasure cruise.

I went back out with the gear in my slicker pocket and stepped up onto the gunwale and grabbed the railing along the edge of the pilothouse. Hanging on as the boat pitched and rolled, I inched out over the cabin on the starboard side. When the rod swung back to starboard I let go a hand and grabbed it. Now to get on top. I let my body figure it out, trusting it. A heave and a leg up over the railing, chest and stomach flat to the roof. I got to my knees, wide-angled, and braced my feet on the handrails. I held the antenna in the dangling bracket with one hand, then had to let go the rail with the other to reach for the long screws in my pocket, holding on with my knees and braced feet as the boat dipped and rolled. It was hard to hold the rod steady and fit the screw into the hole. The rain pelting my face didn't help. Holding the antenna was like holding a giant icicle. My wet hands got cold right off, especially the left hand clasping the antenna. Gloves were out of the question, too clumsy—but would numb hands be any better? The boat rolled and heaved, and my leg muscles trying to grip the roof felt as if they were about to cramp. I froze in place.

Then I was in a strange hiatus. I suddenly felt tired, tired of the struggle. Of all the struggles. I no longer felt the rain stinging my face and hands. The black waves heaved hissing by close to my ear, whispering. From the corner of my eye I watched them, the endless ranks of them rolling with the weight of eternity.

Let go, let go, they whispered, let the black forever waters take you, rocking, swaying, down to silence, down to sweet oblivion, the enfolding dark bliss.

A light fell across my hands: Steve with the flashlight through the windshield. He saw my difficulties, trying to hold the rod and bracket and get the screw seated. He moved out on the port side, holding on to the railing. An anguish of fear for him went through me, but I refused it. With the force of the wind and the lurching boat on the antenna, I needed all the strength in my left hand and arm to hold it in place. Steve put the flashlight in his mouth and with his free hand reached over to help me steady the rod. In the nick of time. My thumb muscle was aching and threatening to quit, my fingers losing the sense of touch. I concentrated on the job, ignoring the various pain signals from my body, and worked as fast as I could, mindful not to drop the screws. Steve held steady. We didn't need to talk. The situation was clear enough. The boat pitched and rolled like a bronco wanting us off its back. The waves hissed by unconcerned. Now with both hands I got the screws started, drove them home, then changed the screwdriver for a crescent wrench and turned the lag bolts down tight on the flange. By then my leg muscles had begun to tremble and fail.

But the rig should hold at least till morning, when we could fix it in place better with an additional bracket from the parts box. We eased back along the gunwale and went below. My hands started thawing, the usual pliers clamping down on each fingertip. No matter. We still had a radio. That was what mattered.

❀

I watched the light move slowly out of the northeast, in no hurry, a calm, pale, austere lady moving gracefully across the sky, lightly touching the sea with color. The rain had stopped, the clouds were lifting, and the wind had calmed down. Our night on the outside was behind us, safe and sound in the network of our memories.

We finished the antenna job, then pulled the net in, picking about another hundred fish. The engine started without protest, and I headed slowly back toward Naknek. We had moved out with the fleet and done all right and seen something. We felt pretty good.

*10*

## THREADING THE NEEDLE

It was very quiet, the only sound was the waves hushing along the hull, rhythmic, very much like surf breaking softly on a distant beach. The engine was off. Steve and I were on a drift. The boat rose and fell gently as each wave passed. Both the sound and the motion should have been soothing, but now the silence and the whispering foam seemed somehow insidious. Stretched out on my bunk, I was supposed to be sleeping, but I was restless, apprehensive. The fog had come on like a woolly blanket drawn slowly over our eyes. All landmarks were blotted out. Gray billows rolled heavily over the water, spreading oblivion, confounding the distinction between sky and sea. Even the radio was silent, as though all the other boats had materially vanished.

The tide was ebbing fast, carrying us along with it. We had laid out in an area off by ourselves well above the mouth of the Naknek River, so I wasn't specifically worried about running afoul of another boat's nets. There had been plenty of open water around us, and everything afloat would be carried along by the tide just as we were, unless anchored. I remembered hearing about some big Japanese processing vessels, cash buyers, supposed to be moored somewhere off the river's mouth on the east side. But I figured we were surely a good way west and above their probable location. Still—there were so many variables.

Steve was up on deck keeping watch. He was quick-minded, quick to react, not given to second-guessing. I trusted his judgment. Still I couldn't relax. The fog had settled like a miasma on my mind, oppressive, dank, muffling. We had laid out two shackles. Okay. That was better than three if for some reason we had to pull in. But maybe it would be best to leave only one out . . . or pull them both in until the fog lifted. I swung my legs out and sat on the edge of the bunk, listening—for what? I pulled on my slippers and went up on deck.

Steve was sitting easy on the captain's stool, gazing out astern, his tanned face a touch of color against the gray of the fog. He turned when he heard my steps.

"It hasn't lifted any," he said. "Might even be a little worse."

I nodded. Even with only two nets out I could no longer see the big orange end buoy. The line of white corks astern grayed and disappeared at about two or three fathoms out. Otherwise there was nothing to be seen or heard beyond the hush of the small circle of water on which we floated, without bearings, in a dimensionless void. I thought of the Eastern idea of fundamental reality as indeed a boundless void, nothing to hold on to, no one to do the holding, a dance of measureless energy in eternal transformation. But I didn't feel much like dancing just then. A gull came out of the mist, glided across our stern and vanished, then reemerged, wheeling back across, as though it, too, were uncertain of its whereabouts and glad to have come across something solid.

Steve, sensing my uneasiness, looked over at me.

"What do you think?"

His question made me decide.

"I think we better pull in till we can see where we're going."

And then the fog started to lift, as unexpectedly as it had come down. It thinned into lacy jags and a breeze came through, parting the veils like curtains being drawn at the start of a play. Rays of the sun glowed and sparkled through the haze, and out of the brilliance, first partially and then altogether, loomed the dark massive silhouettes of two ships and a scow immediately in our path: the Japanese processing vessels, moored to huge steel buoys. The strong tide rolling past made them look as though they were underway, curling the water aside as they bore down on us. For the first instant, the sight filled all of my consciousness and there was no room for a reaction; the ships and the scow were just there, as though an impassive camera had recorded their existence; then a sick constriction went through me as I realized what was happening. Steve stood up and shot me a look.

"Holy shit," I said in something like a whisper.

Without another word we both started for the stern hold. There was no time for boots and slickers or gloves. I grabbed the corkline and Steve the lead line and we both started pulling with all our might and I thought: We'll have bad hands before we're through this.

The net came in fast, spraying water. There were very few fish in the meshes to slow us down. Good. Our bodies charged with adrenaline, for the first minutes our arms pumped like pistons, but then I felt the muscles in my arms, shoulders, and back beginning a familiar hurt, signaling me to slack off a bit. Sorry, muscles, can't be done. Hang in there. This is a case of mind over matter. In response my fingers curled into rigid hooks, and I pulled more with the weight of my body than with the strength of my arms, which had none.

Our end buoy, slightly fishhooked to the net, was sliding right toward the ship's buoy. It looked very close; I couldn't tell for sure. There was nothing to do but keep pulling, get in all the net we could, and hope we scraped by. I was aware of the scow and second ship ahead to our left, but I didn't worry about them. One crisis at a time. First see if we miss the buoy. The ship itself rose up out of the water like a black mountain as we neared. Its white superstructure seemed far above the baleful little drama we were playing out. No one appeared on deck. Maybe no one thought it of sufficient consequence to interrupt whatever they were doing. We wrap the buoy or we slip by. None of their affair. Maybe they were all busy playing cards or burning incense to the Buddha. I thought of Auden's poem about how the old masters were always right in their portrayals of disastrous events, how when Icarus fell out of the sky some farmer nearby was preoccupied with plowing to the end of the row and didn't even notice the pair of legs disappearing into the water.

We swept past with I don't know how many yards or feet or inches to spare. So much for Scylla. Now for Charybdis. It was the fishhook at the end of the net that could snag the ship's sharp bow. But then again maybe that loop back on itself would make the margin of difference, shortening the net just enough. Both of us intently watched the end of the net as we pulled. The scene went into freeze-frame, an interval of timelessness, a suspension. All the world was reduced to a black hull and an orange ball. And then in the next frame the orange ball blazed out against the black hull, and we had missed the bow by what looked like the dimension of the buoy's reflection on the hull.

We didn't waste our breath talking. Nothing needed to be said. The situation was perfectly simple. The ship was a monster, and the scow and the other ship were monsters. We had eluded the first of the three. The second was coming on fast, frothing at the mouth. We pulled harder. I felt I had used up my reserves, was pulling on empty. My muscles were now thinking of mutiny, but my will had become a Captain Bligh: "And would you rather get hung up and sucked under? I think not. Keep at it, you bloody beggars, no quitting now. By Jove!" And this sent another jolt of adrenaline into the battle.

About half of the last shackle was still out, probably just enough to pull us under. I had an idea, something we could try.

"Keep pulling till I start the engine," I said to Steve. "And if we catch the scow, cut the net loose." (Cutting the net loose would not be that easy or fast a job; there were the stout corkline, the webbing, and the lead-cored lead line to deal with.)

Steve nodded, felt behind him for his knife, and kept pulling. I climbed up forward, started the engine, threw it into forward, and turned the wheel hard to starboard. Maybe I could drag the last segment of net back out of reach of the scow. I put as much throttle into it as I dared. Now would not be a good time to blow the engine. Steve stood in the stern watching, knife in hand. The scow was within hailing distance, but there was no one evident to hail. And what could we have said that wasn't obvious? What kind of help could we have called for? If we wrapped them and couldn't cut loose of the net before the *Diane* started listing and taking on water, I supposed they would interrupt whatever they were doing long enough to throw us a line or a life preserver.

But we slipped by, again by a whisker. Good enough! A miss is as good as a mile. The other ship was not directly in our path. We would pass it with room to spare, now that most of the net was on board. We had—by Jove, perhaps—threaded the needle.

We let the last of the net stay in the water and fell back where we stood, Steve on the pile of net and fish in the stern and I on the captain's stool. We drifted in the clear for several minutes, saying nothing, the ships and scow falling away behind us. Then we pulled in the rest of the net and slowly picked the few fish. Even with gloves on now, our hands hurt. It would be a day or so at least before they could be pressed back into service. And as for our muscles, they had signed off and walked out.

The fishing period wasn't over, but I turned our bow back up towards the Naknek. By not making another drift we might miss out on a couple hundred fish, but that was okay. We would just do a bit more hunting that winter.

Some fog still hung over land and sea, but it had thinned into a luminous mist, golden now in the radiance of the setting sun.

❁

An anecdote involving Pope and an Outside boat might illustrate the extreme aversion fishermen have to the prospect of wrapping a scow or ship, especially on a night drift, when both men might be catching a little shut-eye. As is true of most accidents, when it happens it happens fast, sometimes before you even realize it's happening. You could be inhaling saltwater before you rose to the occasion.

Twice earlier in the season the same Outside boat had corked Pope when he had been on a good drift and catching fish. He had hurled a lot of strong language at the other boat on the first occasion, but to no avail. A few days later it happened again. There was little Pope could do to right the wrong or compensate himself for the loss of the fish that should have been his. He was operating a skiff-and-kicker rig (an open boat powered by outboard engines), and the other boat was one of the newer aluminum vessels, so he couldn't muscle it out of the way, and he wasn't quite angry enough to board the boat wielding a harpoon.

Several nights later he made a set he hoped to ride through the darker hours, maybe catch a little sleep, and he noticed the other boat laying out too, not corking him this time but close enough to reawaken his animosity. He stood watching, ruminating. When he saw the cabin light go out after a while, he knew just what to do.

There were a couple of tally scows in the area, which those Outside guys would have noticed. Pope waited a little longer, then turned loose his nets, letting them float on the easy swells until his return. With only one of his twin Mercury outboards purring, he moved in close enough to the tin can, as the aluminum boats were called, so that when he cut the motor he would drift alongside. He held a gigantic wrench in his hand, and when a swell heaved his lighter skiff against the boat he struck with all his might up forward on the metal hull where they would be sleeping, and at the same time he screamed at the top of his lungs: "Tally scow! Tally scow!" Then he added the roar of his engines to the sudden explosion of noise and sped away, his wash rocking the other boat. There was just enough light for Pope, looking back, to see the two terror-stricken figures in long johns burst out on deck to stand dumbfounded, with no scow in sight, only a cruising skiff.

Vengeance is mine, sayeth the Lord. But that night Pope considered himself His chosen vessel.

# 11

# PARTY

All through the fishing season the two bars in Dillingham placed an extra ten-cent tab on every drink: not just on those destined for the fisherman's hollow leg, but on all drinks. Everyone, townspeople and tourists as well as Outside fishermen, coughed up the extra dime. No one complained. Outsiders probably didn't even notice, and the townspeople understood. It was for a worthy cause: to finance D Inn Crowd's annual end-of-the-season party up on Lake Aleknagik. The fishing was over—the sleepless nights, the mind-numbing weariness, the shivering cold, the subliminal terror in face of the ruthless sea. What then? Should the fisherman be content to sit around counting his blessings and dollars? Not D Inn Crowd. For them it was party time, and they would go at it as hard as they went at the fishing.

P. G. Brennan was honorary chairman of D Inn Crowd's board of directors, and he also owned the Willow Tree Inn. No problem levying the extra dime there. Frank Tomalson managed the Sea Inn Bar, and he was also a fisherman. No problem there either. Moreover, it was really a fair, progressive tax. At both establishments fishermen, especially D Inn Crowd fishermen, were the most enthusiastic and tireless clientele. The extra tab per drink was as nothing to men and women harvesting the bounty of Bristol Bay's salmon run, even if it had been a bum year and the coming winter might be lean: It was the moment that counted, and at the moment a dime was nothing. By August those dimes had grown into enough money to throw a very big party.

The Sunday-morning meetings of the board at the Willow Tree also contributed to the cause. The twelve-member board was made up of the elite of the elite Inn Crowd. As secretary I was charged with keeping the minutes. The board met on Sunday mornings at the Willow because it was convenient: Most of the members had been on the premises since the night before. There was no way these meetings could get serious. My minutes read like the script of a Marx Brothers movie:

Johanson jumps to his feet, without having gotten Chairman Jackson's permission to take the floor.

"I object to that, Jackson!" he protests. "You didn't have a majority on that."

Chairman Jackson stands, or sits, firm. "Okay, Johanson, that'll be a ten-spot for speaking out of order." He motions to Kenny Brandon, sergeant at arms. "Collect that in cash, Mr. Brandon. No IOUs."

Johanson explodes. "What?!" His black hair spikes, his black beard bristles. "You can't—I had my hand up! *You're* out of order!"

"Brother Johanson," the chairman responds mildly, "at meetings of the board I'm not *Jackson*. I'm 'Mister Chairman.' So that's—"

"*Mister*, my ass."

"—another five on top of the ten. A little respect for proper procedures is needed around here."

Danny looks fierce, is about to protest further, but then breaks into a smile.

"Shit, I say." He reaches into his jeans and pulls out a ten and a five, which Kenny collects with tilted eyebrows and drops into the beige jar in the center of the table. Danny pours himself another glass of champagne and sits down. All the brothers look happy.

To tell the truth, D Inn Crowd, despite its honorific "board of directors" and the punctuality of its meetings, was really an informal, not to say loose, affiliation of the more prestigious or notorious fishermen whose sole purpose was to alter their body chemistry in such a way and to such a degree as to produce the highest-intensity and longest-lasting euphoria possible. D Inn Crowd was a drinking and partying fraternity dedicated to bliss, hit or miss.

The main business of the board meetings was to go over preparations for the big party, although voting on the induction of honorary tundra bunnies was also important. The meetings often lasted all morning. Instead of coffee, which would have given succor and comfort to sobriety, a magnum of champagne and a tall-stemmed glass were placed before each member. As a result *Robert's Rules of Order* were not always strictly adhered to. Each violation of board-meeting etiquette was, as noted, fined ten dollars, to be collected on the spot by Kenny, who carried a purely symbolic black zap in his back pocket. Each meeting thus swelled the treasury by at least a hundred dollars and sometimes more, when, halfway through, the rules changed from Robert's to Jackson's and Kenneth's. The wholesale champagne thus paid for itself.

As mentioned previously, the conclusion of the 1967 season, when I flew up to Dillingham alone, a veteran of four years' fishing and partying, the year Pope and I fished together as partners on the *Diane* and made seventh high boat (with me as captain, no less), remains in my mind the most memorable and representative of the end-of-the-season parties and the triumphant conclusion of my long effort to prove up as a fisherman and an hombre.

Preparations had been in the works for weeks. Jackson handled most of the arrangements. That is, he arranged to purchase the cases of champagne, scotch, bourbon, whiskey, wine, beer, and soda that would float our bark of mayhem to the other side. A few of the ladies associated by marriage or adoption with D Inn Crowd saw to it that enough salmon (to be split and nailed to a driftwood board and broiled by an open fire), a side or two of beef (roasted on a spit), hamburger by the kilo, and hot dogs by the gross arrived at the party site in good order. Even P. G.'s Indians (which was another name for D Inn Crowd) didn't live by booze alone, although they sometimes tried.

No other arrangements were necessary. We wouldn't have to reserve a hall because the party would take place in the open air of Lake Aleknagik. We wouldn't need a license or permit because there weren't that many people in the area to generate those kinds of rules. Bristol Bay was only half tamed. Rules and regulations were waiting for the man who shot Liberty Valance.

A dirt, gravel, and mud road connected Dillingham with the village of Aleknagik, situated on the shores of the lake where it drains into the Wood River, which in turn empties into Nushagak Bay near Dillingham. The village was owned and operated by a society of Seventh-Day Adventists, very clean-living, sober folks. This settlement was not, to be sure, the proposed site of the party. (The lion does not yet lie down with the lamb, unless the lamb is in its belly.) The party would merely pass by the neat white-frame buildings on its way to the mouth of the Agulowok River, about twenty miles farther north.

❈

The Wood River chain of lakes, of which Aleknagik is the first, ascends into virgin country north of Dillingham, each lake linked to the next by a river—more exactly, by a large trout stream. These lakes are considerable bodies of water, Aleknagik running perhaps forty miles long and a mile or so wide. Besides the village, there were then only a few scattered dwellings in the whole region, mostly down close to the village. Big John

Pierson, a very large and mostly uncouth bush rat noted for having blown fifty grand in two weeks in Seattle, operated a sport-fishing camp halfway up the Agulowok and enjoyed out-fishing his clientele.

These lakes and rivers were cold and clear. You might step off in what appeared to be a foot of water and find yourself in over your head. Major spawning grounds for the Bristol Bay salmon pack, these waters also held trophy rainbow trout, arctic char, northern pike, and grayling. Sport fishing for these species, especially in the connecting rivers, couldn't be beat anywhere in the world, and you wouldn't be standing shoulder to shoulder on opening day or any other day, unless with a curious bear or slow-thinking moose.

When the salmon were spawning, arctic char schooled up off the mouths of the rivers by the hundreds to lie in wait for the eggs drifting down to them. More than once I stood in the stern of *Port N Storm* and caught five-pound char, in the fall closely resembling the eastern brook trout, until my arms tired, using just a Daredevl spoon with a single barbless hook, so they could be released without harm. It seemed to work that wherever the gulls and terns were milling and diving, usually just off from where the river current dropped into deep water, the char were massed, the biggest ones lying deepest. Of course, the birds were having a salmon-egg orgy too.

Whereas the land around Nushagak Bay and the Naknek/ Kvichak watershed was mostly flat, treeless tundra, the Wood River Lakes country was forested and mountainous. It was the kind of strikingly beautiful country that has inspired painters and photographers for so long its reproduced image has become a stereotype. But it was nevertheless magnificent, in the large and rawboned way typical of the Alaskan landscape.

That year, three of us ran up the Wood River together: Pope and I on the *Diane*, Kenny and Louie on the *Wanda B*, and Danny and his partner Chucky Nunn, known as the Pelican, on a really tough ship whose name I can't remember. I'll call it the

*Bilgewater* because it was always half full of water and on the verge of sinking, even though it was a relatively new boat with a rotating periscope rig below that allowed the captain to survey the scene above while reclining in his bunk. Maybe that was how the troubles with the boat began.

For at least a third of the way up to Aleknagik the Wood River is tidal and opaque gray. Two or even three fish boats can run abreast easily on the flood so long as the man at the wheel knows or can read the channels. Even as the water clears and shows bottom, the tide will still affect its depth, if you've caught a big flood at the right time. But it would be foolish, though maybe possible, for two boats to try to navigate the upper reaches tied together. The bottom is close to the top and strewn with unforgiving boulders. We were transporting several cases of the booze and of course had begun sampling the stuff in transit, but this time about halfway up we cut loose and went Indian file, as was prudent.

Other fish boats and skiffs had gone up before us, and several more would follow. The big flat-bottomed skiffs could run the river at any time, like water bugs. P. G. was to lead a small caravan of cars up the road, his jeep wagon loaded down with party gear and tundra bunnies. As we steamed around the last bend of the river into the lake, we spotted his contingent waiting over by the beach, several cars and scattered groups of figures watching us approach. An ordinary entrance was out of the question.

Kenny and Danny were ahead of Gene and me, and when the *Wanda B* poured on the coal, sprouting a rooster's tail, so did the *Bilgewater*. They were wide open, knifing directly toward the beach.

"Sock it to her, captain," said Pope. "We also must make a proper entrance."

So the three boats were up on the step and bearing straight down on the beach like P. T. boats making a hit.

They watched us coming. Then a bunch of girls started jumping around and waving. P. G. hopped into the wagon, spun a brodie on the gravel, and backed halfway into the lake. As though the maneuver had been rehearsed, Kenny headed for the jeep full tilt, then at the last minute simultaneously kicked his engine into hard reverse and spun the wheel. The *Wanda B* stopped on a dime and lightly drifted broadside up to the rear of the wagon.

Danny repeated the maneuver, neatly settling next to the *Wanda B*.

Boats were to those guys what choppers are to bikers.

I started to follow suit, even if the suit might not fit. As the *Diane* bore down on the scene with me at the helm and close enough to be recognized, everyone pretended to panic. I was still a little green in their eyes. The Nicholson brothers jumped into their skiff and sped out of the way. Girls ran screaming up the beach, waving their arms, glossy black hair flying. Kenny and Louie and Danny and Chucky jumped up onto the gunwales of their boats and made as if they were about to abandon ship.

Pope leaped up to the bow and waved his arms frantically for them to get out of the way, then quick as a cat was at my side.

"Now, Professor," he said quietly and hit the throttle as hard as was needed while I threw her into reverse and spun the wheel. We settled right beside the *Bilgewater*.

Everybody cheered. Bunnies jumped up and down with glee. Pope and I bowed and shook hands.

While the girls and assorted brothers scrambled aboard the boats, the rest of us loaded the remaining booze and food on board. There was a lot of booze. If at least a hundred dedicated drinkers didn't show, it would be a long session for the faithful, because it was a creed in outback Alaska that a party didn't end until the booze did.

Weather in Bristol Bay tends to be contrary, brooding: overcast squally spells with clouds the color of a bruise and sudden downpours mixed with washes of humid sunshine; or it can sock in solid and drizzle for so long people have to spray themselves with fungicide to keep from developing mold. Everything about Alaska is excessive. (But then, as Blake said, "The road of excess leads to the palace of wisdom.")

But this day was fair. Great white cumulus clouds billowed up from behind the mountains rimming the lake, and a fresh breeze whitecapped the open reaches of water. The sun sparkled off the bow spray of the three boats cruising up the blue lake together and glinted off the bottles and glasses in the passengers' hands.

Kenny and Danny stood at the wheel of the *Wanda B*, talking and drinking. They had doffed their shirts, two swarthy, broad-shouldered men. They were at home in this country, had been born and raised here, as had their fathers and mothers. On the native side of their bloodlines their connection with the land went back a very long way. "Brandon" and "Johanson" are not indigenous names, of course, but their broad, powerful backs spoke of their heritage.

All these men around me were tough, in the true sense of the word. Physically strong, inured to hardship and danger, they could take what the country dished out, which could be a lot. But the confluence of native culture and the white man's civilization sometimes produced tide rips in their psyches. Several of the hombres wandering among the three boats had in the past erupted into forms of violence incompatible with the law. Johanson, for instance, had done time for assault and battery. I never saw him in a fight and was glad of that. But as for tough, I will remember the gray blustery day near the outside markers of Nushagak Bay when Pope and I spotted the *Bilgewater* adrift and getting knocked around. At our approach Danny and Chucky appeared on deck in boots and shirtsleeves, both of them with week-old beards. Two men standing spread-legged on a piece of wood in the middle of the ocean. They had been on the water for days and were now broken down without power, drifting out with the tide, the only boat around. (I forget what brought Pope and me out that far, having to buck tide back; I think we were looking for a shackle of gear we had lost the night before when we untied from it briefly to visit with Jerry Nicholson, who had been drifting nearby.)

Did they need any help?

"No sweat, man," Danny yelled back. "Save us a couple of beers at the Willow."

They stood there for a minute after we pulled away. I imagined them below, slopping around in the bilgewater, deliberately going about fixing the engine.

Danny's partner, Chucky—the Pelican—was a big muscular fellow. Always good-natured and never a wise guy when I knew him, he had nevertheless earned a reputation somewhere along the line. I recall Kenny interrupting us quietly one time when we had been ribbing Chucky. "Better knock it off," he had said. "I think he's getting negative." Nobody was inclined to put the diagnosis to the test.

And across from me, sitting on the gunwales in a T-shirt, taking a long belt out of one of the bottles, was Johnny Larson. A smart fisherman and something of a loner in his mid-twenties, Johnny owned and operated a top-of-the-line hull fitted with a reel—a big power-driven spool that wound in the net while he picked fish, so that one man could fish alone. It was as recently as the last bash at the Sea Inn that I had seen Johnny being pulled away from a fight with his shirt ripped into shreds, his right arm and clenched fist exposed and swinging at his side like a sledgehammer.

A full description of these partygoers, now already well lubricated with booze, that known agitator of violence, would read like a rogue's gallery. I had seen the jovial native turn sullen and mean before, in direct proportion to the booze consumed. Why shouldn't he? It's not hard to understand. The goddamn white man just barges in and takes over everything with his greed and lies. Goddamn white man! Everywhere he goes he destroys the free natural people and the wild animals and lays waste the land.

As I watched those macho Indians swallowing all that fire-water, I suffered a down spell of paranoia. What was I doing among these people, I the middle-class white intellectual? They could really have no use for me. I was an intruder from another, suspect world, kind of slumming, as it were. Under their affability they harbored a generic resentment. I could easily wind up with my teeth or an eye knocked out or my nose or head bashed in.

And here I was, cozying up to Arlene, the Eskimo wife of one of them, who was off doing something somewhere in Alaska. That was sure to endear me to their brotherly affections. The goddamn white man not only steals my fish, he wants my women.

When the bottle came my way I downed a good belt. Well, after all, the hell with it, I thought, in a sudden revulsion at my paranoia. You can't go around worrying about things like that. Sink or swim. He who seeks to save his life will lose it.

I stood up and took off my shirt, handing it to Arlene with a smile—would she hold it for me for a minute?

These fish boats did not cater to creature comforts. They had no head. Everything went over the side directly or indirectly. The country was immense and the people few, so pollution wasn't a problem yet. Will a wild bear shit in the woods?

The three boats were knifing through the water at a good clip, keeping pace with the mood of their passengers. I stepped up onto the gunwale in the stern, beside the power roller, a precarious perch. Below me the water was churned white by the propellers. With my back to everyone, I started taking a free-hand leak as my eyes swept along the mountains.

The top of one of the mountains stopped my eyes dead in their tracks. The configuration of rock and snow formed a gigantic visage, an ancient craggy face, dispassionate as the Buddha but at the same time stern, almost ghoulish, no hint of a reassuring smile, no trace of compassion toward a frail humanity. It returned my gaze steadily, seemed concentrated intently on me. As the boat moved, its cavernous eyes followed me. This face came from someplace beyond pleasure and pain, life and death. It spoke to me without words, a meaning as immediate as sight. It rebuked my fear and confirmed my impulse to dare: because nobody dies.

When I sat down by Arlene again I took another swig of whiskey and was ready to party.

❖

Where the Agulowok River enters Lake Aleknagik has been the site of a fish camp since remote times. The wooden frames for holding the split salmon were weathered silver and stretched out along the gravel beach like the bones of a dinosaur. This was the spot chosen for our party. The sun was behind the mountains now, and dusk was coming on fast.

Several skiffs and fish boats were nosed into the beach near where big driftwood fires blazed. As we approached we could make out a couple of dozen figures moving about, some of the men in white caps lit by the firelight. Up a ways from the mouth of the river shone the orange lights of Bill Miner's cabin; more boats were tied up there.

Our three-boat flotilla would not be the last to arrive, but most of the heavyweights were on board, including P. G. himself: P. G. Brennan, besides owning the Willow Tree, a cannery boss, a tall, slow-talking southern transplant with charisma. He kept a jug in his desk drawer, knowing his fishermen, and plied it as occasion warranted. The fishermen liked him, he was a fair and classy boss—not actually a boss, of course, since most salmon fishermen are their own men, work for themselves and sell to the canneries. But as often as not the relationship degenerates into something like sharecropping. The fishermen get into hock to the cannery for boats, nets, engines, repairs, and so forth. So the cannery boss has power. But P. G. wasn't known to use his clout unfairly, and he was never out of reach. That's what the jug in the drawer said.

We nosed into the beach, and the party officially began. The boxes of food and the cases of mind benders and libido releasers were unloaded. Some of the women started right in on the salmon, squatting on their heels as they worked, in the old posture. Most of the partygoers were already in the land of here and now, living in the present tense.

❖

With a jug in each hand, the Professor steps up onto the bow of the *Diane*. He has been readying himself all the way up the Wood River and all the way down Lake Aleknagik, and now he is ready. His shirt is gone, and although the night air is chilly, he doesn't feel it. He wears old jeans and fisherman's slippers, and his cap is low over his eyes. Holding his arms out, jugs in hand, he yells "Geronimo!" and jumps down onto the beach. The beach, however, is farther away than he had reckoned, and his balance isn't as good as it had once been. His feet hit the gravel squarely a few inches shoreward of the water's edge, but the rest of him is not quite perpendicular, is in fact leaning astern. Gravity is on the job. He plops back, sitting in about six inches of cold lake water, and despite the gasping shock of it enjoys the roar of laughter that goes up. He remains there, knees up, arms and bottles outstretched, maintaining a sitting posture but unable to get up.

Danny swaggers over. "Jesus Christ, Prop. What are we gonna do with you? It's only the first day, and look at you." He reaches out and pulls the Professor up with one arm (fishermen who pull in nets loaded with fish get big arms).

The Professor backs up to a fire, warming up, drying his jeans. He pulls on a jug and feels a hand run across his shoulders.

Arlene is next to him. He knows she likes him. She's intellectually inclined and wants to pick an argument with him whenever she gets a little juiced. Sober, she's reserved, distant, in another world. He turns to meet her eyes, which are half closed, not just from drinking; it's an attitude, taunting, challenging.

"You trying to cool yourself off, Professor?" She glances down at his wet jeans, pasted to his butt.

"Well, if I was it wouldn't work now." He looks at her sideways and grins.

She bumps him with her shoulder. "You're cute," she says.

He can see she's no more than a drink or two away from drunk, and he knows what she's like in that condition. One night late at the Willow they had danced, call it the pelvic grind. She was strong and held him tightly to her, her head back and to one side, her heavy-lidded eyes fixed on him, regarding him as though in mockery. Her full lips parted somewhere between a smile and a sneer.

"You think you're so smart because you're a professor."

There she went again, picking a fight. But he remembered reading about the old Eskimo ways, something about courtship conducted like a skirmish, chasing and catching, wrestling and throwing down, biting and scratching, wanting but resisting. This was 1967, she was educated, lived in a modern apartment, had a washer and dryer, but here she was in the darkness of the dance hall an Eskimo woman, direct, forceful, playing the old games.

"Smart enough," he said back.

She kissed him and held his lower lip between her teeth, looking into his eyes.

He pulled away, aggravated; her teeth had hurt. The music took a turn, he felt the movement, went with it, and swung her about so that his thigh pressed between hers and he could feel the bulge. And the heat of it. He shifted and pushed hard against her.

When they sat down in the dark booth, just dim red lights

on the walls and ceiling, Pope came over with a guitar and a microphone on a long cable. "Come on, Professor, sing us a song." The Professor was drunk and high and feeling careless, invulnerable, muffled away in some cool observing place. Arlene was behind him, next to the wall. She took the mike, pressing against him, and held it for him so he could strum the guitar. He started a Dylan song, somewhat startled to hear his voice come back so loud through the speakers. *I'll be your baby tonight.*

Though it was late, the Willow was still crowded. Some danced; at the tables and bar others talked or listened, glancing in his direction now and then. They all knew him. The Professor. When he finished the song, having garbled some of the verses, he held the guitar with his left hand, smiling at the applause, and with his right hand he reached back between her legs. The jukebox started again, some boozy slow number packing the dance floor with bodies undulating in a syrup of sex. They made out in the back of the booth, grappling like a couple of mollusks on the ocean floor. Everybody knew but nobody noticed. This was the underworld, where names and addresses were forgotten.

It had gone no further. Her husband, a mild and sober guy the Professor knew a little, showed up to take her home. If he ran into her the next day on the streets of Dillingham, it would have been as if they never had met.

❁

"Hey, Prop, we need more fish. Come on, show us where they hang out. Show us how to do it."

It's Danny Johanson, not to be denied. Danny is tickled to think that this civilized professor dude, his friend, knows where the fish are.

They start up the trail toward Miner's cabin, where the *Bil-*

*gewater* is parked. The Professor looks back. Arlene is standing by the fire watching them. He will see more of her before this party winds down. The land of shopping carts is far away.

The nights are still short the first week of August, and the day is starting to break. A good hour to go fishing.

The Professor is at the wheel. They all know he has lived on Lake Nerka, the second of the Wood River Lakes, and has fished the mouth of the Agulowok many times. Kenny somehow is on board, too, and Dutch, a mean-eyed bastard and brawny, with a reputation for breaking jaws. Carla and Irene, two good-looking young girls just old enough to be at this party, also climb on board.

The current in front of Miner's cabin runs swift and strong, impatient to get to the lake. The Professor will have to maneuver the *Bilgewater* back down with the current to get to where the fish are, where the river empties into the lake and the water is deep. But his head is divorced from pragmatics. He can see and feel fine, even wondrously, but he can't calculate well. Running up a river isn't so bad; you can feel your way against the current, bow first, with nice control. But how do you get back down? In reverse somehow? Bow first, stern first? He remembers hitting the Kvichak behind Pope: like a runaway train. Control is what you need. He ponders the problem, to no avail.

"Let's shove off, Captain," says Kenny.

Okay. Danny and Dutch undo the lines. The Professor turns the wheel, the current grabs the boat, and they are off and running, backward (not so good, the prop exposed to the boulders). He throttles forward, trying to slow down.

"All wrong, Professor. You're doing it all wrong."

That was Dutch. Uh-oh. But never blink an eye. The Professor clasps one of the girls around the waist and takes another pull on the jug, trying to think clearly, trying to think at all. The girl is so small and delicate.

"No sweat, Dutch. Hang on, we're under way."

The captain is grinning, and his eyebrows are up to at least a thirty-degree angle of nonchalance, one hand on the wheel, his arm around the girl's adorably slender waist.

"Yeah. Show us how it's done, Prop," Danny laughs (this is his Professor boilerplate).

Kenny is shaking his head and chuckling. "You fuckin' farmer."

They make it out of the river, and the Professor is pleasantly surprised that they make it but still trying to imitate nonchalance, when the boat lurches and grinds to a stop on the gravel shoal hooking out from the river's mouth.

"Every man for himself!" Kenny shouts.

He flips off his slippers and jumps over the side. He stands in about two feet of water and shoves against the hull. Danny and Dutch join him. The girl is squirming in the Professor's embrace. The *Bilgewater* moves, the current takes her, and they are off again. Kenny, Danny, and Dutch grab hold of the tire bumpers on the side and climb back on board.

The Professor stays at the wheel and maneuvers into position where the birds are wheeling and diving, white flashes against the sky, screeching like banshees. They catch a dozen big char in as many minutes. The fish are in their fall colors, red spots along the flanks, white and orange edges to their fins: full-bodied, small-headed, good fish.

Back on the beach, bonfires blaze, and it looks like a witches' sabbath, silhouetted figures leaping and dancing. Pope is banging the guitar and singing in his booming voice about the sloop *John B*, but nobody as yet looks so broke up they want to go home.

❀

In the old days, according to story and myth, when kings ruled more conspicuously than the wealthy do now, they sometimes disguised themselves as ordinary mortals in order to eavesdrop

BOB DURR

undetected among the commoners. It was a form of slumming similar to getting a swell party together and crossing to the wrong side of the Thames to catch a little bawdy at the Globe.

Were such a modern-day prince—a David Rockefeller, say— to don democratic jeans and T-shirt to stand with us aboard the *Bilgewater* as we approached the beach, he would very likely experience some misgivings.

It's not just that so many of the dancing figures are not altogether clothed, neither male nor female, nor that they dance rather strangely, with a kind of abandon, around two blazing fires. Our princely proponent of the American work ethic could explain away most of that by recalling that after all it's still summer and this is—is it not?—a beach party. A little R and R after work is good for productivity. Beach parties are quite normal, really. But there is that about the dancers, some troubling impression slipping through the gridwork of the prince's mind, a gestalt aimed at the old solar plexus, that he cannot quite situate comfortably in a beach movie. There is an effluvium about this scene that stimulates the suspicion that something more or other than civil recreation is at large and heading straight for the night of first ages.

To the third eye it would be apparent that the old god has made his appearance, that it's his shadow that forms and disintegrates on the thrashing willows, his voice that blows in the wind, his musk—odor of goat—that mixes with the dancers' sweat and the woodsmoke, his darkness that shines through their eyes, his exuberance that pulses through their laughter.

Walpurgis Night, a little tardy. A late summer night's dream.

Right into Shakespeare's time, festivals occurred under Christian auspices (and noses) that scholarly hindsight detects to have been originally pre-Christian, perhaps prehistoric, but definitely pagan. Those May Day celebrations, for instance: That pole the virgins danced around so energetically originally signified something more than a stick of wood. It seems that ordinary men and women would, for a night or two, leave behind them the villages and crossroads, also their names and addresses, and with flowers in their hair run amok in the woods. While the rising moon beamed, the rising moral minority of the day, then called Puritans (who settled our country and our hash), were aghast, despite the fact that the villagers always returned to do the laundry and toe the familial line, perhaps a little perkier than before, a bit more elemental.

Nevertheless, were David standing beside us as we touch the beach, he would certainly not disembark, for just then Pope, saying no more than "Watch this," with a gleam of teeth, grabs the squirt can he uses to prime a cranky carburetor and, leaping like a goat out of the shadows, quick as a literal flash gives each of the fires a squirt as he races by.

> *Fire on the mountain*
> *Run boys run*
> *Devil's in the house of the rising sun*

"Pope! You crazy son of a bitch!"

P. G. himself is erupting from a cozy driftwood niche by the second fire, shaking his fist in classical form after the disappearing figure of Gene Pope. He looks around quickly. A couple of bunnies had screamed, more in surprise than fear or pain; a couple of guys besides P. G. had called after Pope, but no one appears to be hurt, no more than a little singed hair and wool. P. G. returns to his young lady, who is sitting there with the sleeping bag clutched to her chin. The incident wasn't all that unusual for P. G. or P. G.'s Indians, and it gave the girls a chance to panic.

Pope's little prank actually sparks the party, so to speak.

For reasons unexplained, the Professor finds himself following Pope up the dark and narrow trail through the dense alders to Bill Miner's cabin. His legs ride along on top of his feet like passengers in a Greyhound bus. The ground moves mysteriously beneath him, effortlessly. The air is cool and pungent with damp earth. The broad alder leaves flap against his face like kisses. By the time he sees the cabin and hears voices, the inflammatory incident on the beach is nothing but a particularly bright circuit in the network of his mind. The present moment seems to be a quantum perpetually unfolding out of nothing.

Bill Miner's one-room cabin holds as many people as can sit or stand, some coming in, some going out. The Professor knows most of them, at least by sight. There's no telling what all the talk and laughing is about. The light is fuzzy in the cigarette smoke. Seats are scarce. The one in the corner by the table that the Professor is sitting on holds two, himself and on his lap Arlene (for she appeared upon the scene shortly after the Professor and went right over to him). Pope and Carla sit across from them. Arlene is drunk but not sloppy. Everyone is drunk but feeling good. The Professor leans across the table to catch what Pope is saying, and Arlene nips the lobe of his ear.

"Quit that, goddammit!"

The Professor feels a flush of anger. Pope watches. Arlene's weight is soft but insistent.

Pope and the Professor keep on talking earnestly, the drink bringing out their liking for each other. Pope's eyes flick back and forth from the Professor to Arlene. He is enjoying the thing going on between them, watching for developments. He has known Arlene and her husband for years. It doesn't matter. Everything that just happens is okay now. If there are complications they come later, in the shopping world.

Arlene slips her hand down under the Professor's belt and pinches his ass hard. The pain and his reaction are simultaneous. He stands up abruptly, dumping her onto the floor. "Goddammit!" he cries again. She glares up at him, her chin thrust out. Her black hair is slick and glossy as silk. He pulls her to her feet and stoops under her middle, throws her over his shoulder and starts across the floor with her, bumping against people standing or dancing.

"Caveman!" Pope shouts after them. Carla says, "Hey!"

He carries her out to the edge of the bushes and lets her down, falling himself, taking her with him to the ground, pulling at her blouse, popping buttons. She glowers at him, breathing hard but saying nothing.

※

Later, hunched by the fire, the Professor eats broiled king salmon in great steaming chunks and washes it down with red wine. He had slept a little with Arlene in the bushes, how long he has no idea, nor does he have any idea where she is now. Maybe she left. A couple of skiffs had gone back. He doesn't try to keep track of anything. The moment takes care of itself, and he goes along for the ride. Time is irrelevant, it is always now in the land where everything is as it is. So simple. When hungry, eat. When tired, rest.

It has begun to drizzle lightly, delicate points of cold on his back. He feels it as from a distance and doesn't mind. No one's spirits dampen. Some dance by the big fires to music from a radio. Others sit around eating and drinking and talking, and some make out in sleeping bags at the edge of the firelight. Pope is nowhere apparent. The Professor thinks he might be in one of those sleeping bags with the girl from Nondalton who had sat by him earlier when he was singing and playing the guitar. (Teresa is mad at him about something or other and won't come to the party.) Or maybe he has crashed on the *Diane*. Not likely: Pope never crashed in the middle of a party, not while the booze supply lasted. But the idea of the *Diane* and his bunk now appeals to the Professor. He's suddenly very tired. So down the beach he goes. For an instant, when he climbs aboard, the old fish and engine smells bring him down a bit: a whiff of the dismal science. But then when he goes below he brightens again. There are bodies in the two bunks, and they are all female. He kicks off his slippers and slips out of his jeans and tries to squirm into his bunk. The two bodies already there squirm too and make petulant, sleepy sounds of protest. It's a very tight fit, but he is really tired, and then his hand touches something fine and he sees a face. It is Bunny Big Boobs, also from Nondalton. She wriggles and pushes his hand away. The other woman grumbles and crawls out of the bunk, muttering as she stumbles up the steps. He can stretch out a little now, and it feels so good he forgets about Bunny Big Boobs and everything else and never finds out if she meant to push his hand away.

Sometime later as his eyes open he realizes he has been hearing someone talking to him. He sees the bottle first. It's right before his eyes, bigger than life and somewhat refracted.

"You better take a good pull on this before you try getting up."

Pope's voice. He's standing there with the tight-lipped smile on, thrusting the bottle of Jack Daniel's toward him, probably wondering what it is about ordinary mortals that makes them want to sleep when there's a party going on.

That was the way D Inn Crowd operated. They never gave the enemy a chance to counterattack and gain a beachhead. Sooner or later they would be overrun because by sheer weight of numbers the enemy was stronger, but they would rather it be later than sooner. Anciently, among the Romans, this mode of operation was known as *carpe diem,* and it is similar to the early Christian idea of taking no thought for the morrow.

And so the party went on for three days and nights, day becoming night, night becoming day. By the morning of the fourth day, however, even the diehards had run down. There was no juice left to start up again. Most of the revelers had collected what they could of themselves and gone back to the world of Laundromats. Only the hard core of D Inn Crowd remained, trying to adjust to the new regime, paying the fiddler. Three of the younger, more durable bunnies slept below.

We sat around on the *Diane* and *Wanda B,* talking fitfully, wondering how much the fiddler would want for the dance. The sun rattled into the sky like a hubcap.

"Okay, mates." Kenny got up. His hair was still combed back as slick as Elvis's. A remarkable man, Kenny. "I'll go build us a pot of coffee." He went below, the only one of us willing to endure the pain of such a violent move. The brazen rays of the sun pierced my closed eyelids like fine needles. Kenny emerged with a big pot of black coffee and some mugs. He knowingly filled the mugs only halfway, but still most of the coffee splashed out before it reached lips.

"Here, Prop, try this," Danny said after I yelled when the hot coffee burned my shaky hand. He pulled one end of a towel around his neck with his left hand, grasped the mug and the other end of the towel in his right, and thus steadied, hoisted the coffee carefully to his lips.

Pope was the only one of us not suffering. He claimed to enjoy hangovers. He said they put him into a weird place that he liked. The one place Pope didn't like was normal reality: Anything was better than that.

The coffee did no good. It was outclassed. We all knew that that much of a hangover could be dealt with only by fighting fire with fire—the hair of the dog.

We started back for Dillingham, the three boats tied together running down Lake Aleknagik, the day being calm. The gulls and terns still hung off the mouth of the Agulowok, looking healthy, full of energy, and free of pain. A bottle of Jack Daniel's appeared to be making the rounds, for humanitarian purposes. Things started mellowing out pretty quickly.

As we entered the Wood River, passing the village of Aleknagik on the right, no one made a move to separate the three boats. The *Diane* was in the middle, and I was at the wheel, steering for all three boats. I don't know why it was that I so often wound up at the wheel. The rocks, seemingly only inches under the surface, didn't make me as nervous as they should have. One fish boat in the river is tricky; three abreast is against the odds. Kenny and Louie sat on the gunwales passing a bottle back and forth. Danny and the Pelican lounged in the stern, sharing another jug and going over the party. Pope stood next to me gazing ahead but really watching the images in his mind. Well, I thought, if they're not worried, why should I be? They're the sailors. I'm just a fuckin' farmer.

I had run this river several times in *Port N Storm*. Some of the channels I remembered; the others I was confident I could read. What bothered me a little was that I was now about four times wider than *Port N Storm*.

Nevertheless, just taking it easy in the morning sun, still lightly nipping on the bottle, the Pelican stretched out asleep, the girls still dreaming below, Kenny idly watching, at one bend of the river moving over to the wheel of the *Wanda B* to help me make the turn, Gene pointing out an occasional marker, we chugged around the last point of land into the Nushagak and tied up at the cannery dock without so much as a scratched hull or nervous stomach.

Running the river I wasn't drunk, but I certainly wasn't sober either. It was an unusual in-between place, cool as a cucumber but alert as a rabbit. It was a place that didn't seem to care. For instance, I didn't care that I had lost my shirt, pants, socks, and slippers and was dressed in someone else's swim trunks, a bit too loose, and that the slippers on my feet were both lefties, neither one my own. Nobody else looked normal either. There were a lot of bare feet and backs on board.

We decided that what we needed now were some charcoal-broiled steaks at the Willow Tree Inn, each one costing the price of an Oldsmobile. So what. In those days we reckoned each fish over the roller at about a dollar. Some days there were two thousand of them.

Inside the Willow was a perpetual gloaming. Outside it might be broad reality, but here it was inside the head when the head is dreaming. There were no windows to the outside world, no harsh daylight speaking of jobs and mortgages, no glare from the metallic ranks of things that must be done. The lights were soft and dim, the music never-never land. An oasis of ease amid the surrounding desert of stress.

The steaks arrived like magic on special platters that kept them sizzling. No one seemed to notice our strange attire. They all knew us, and knew about the party. The little waitress, a pretty Eskimo girl, was bright with interest, looking at us furtively as she served us. Pope and I might as well have been Butch Cassidy and the Sundance Kid. The others in the place glanced at us now and then and smiled at one another. It was pleasant being famous among the bars.

Recovery, however, took days. I found myself lying atop a bed in someone's apartment trying to sleep. I kept my eyes shut, but I couldn't slow down my metabolism, which was running for its life. Not butterflies but leather-winged bats beat around the walls of my stomach, my heart thought I was falling off a cliff, and in my head the projection machine was locked into fast rewind.

Paying the fiddler. I now realized the harlequin who had mastered the ceremonies had horns under his foolscap. Most probably not Satan himself but his man Beelzebub, Lord of the Flies. Had it been possible to get drowsy, the flies buzzing and landing on me would have made it impossible to sleep. What? Did they think I was dead or dying?

Better just to get up and walk around until I run out of gas and fall into a ditch.

Pope, on the other bed, stirred, got up. He looked at me. "No good, eh, Bob? Well, fuck it, why suffer? Come on, let's go get a beer."

Postponing the inevitable. The primrose path to the everlasting headache.

"Yeah, go ahead, Gene. I need a few minutes to get it together."

When he left, one stern and sober thought emerged from the crowd of crazies whirling around in my head: I must not miss my plane back to New York and my family.

They will start up again, for sure, and they will want me with them.

Hide.

The thing to do was disappear. Hole up like a wounded worm.

I left the apartment cautiously. Outside, daylight was a huge aluminum sheet crackling in the wind.

My plan was simple. If I could make my way undetected to the Stovalls' place on the hill, I'd be safe. They wouldn't be likely to look for me there. Jay and Katie would understand. Their little house and garden glowed in my mind like a sanctuary. Oh, the good, sane, dear sober workaday people—how I envied them. I vowed to be like them, to join ranks with them. No more Dionysian devilry.

Jay was off flying some clients somewhere, but Katie was home. She appeared at the door like a ministering angel. Alaska born and bred and having lived in Dillingham for years, she didn't need an explanation. One look at me told her everything. And she had heard about the party, was even half expecting me—I had taken refuge with the Stovalls before.

Their daughter, Sam, was away. Her little bedroom in the back was available. Katie smiled and ran her hand through her iron-gray hair. Could she get me anything? Would anything help? Some tomato juice?

Nothing helped. I lay there on Sam's ruffled bed, hearing the kids outside in the normal world, watching the sunlight move across the dresser, waiting for time to do the healing. I must have dozed off a little. A car pulling up snapped me to. There were voices. Shit! They've found me, I'll never make it out of Dillingham alive, never get back to my little farm and family.

But I heard wise Katie telling them, "No, he hasn't come by here. I'll let him know if I see him." The engine started and the car pulled away. Maybe I would make it after all.

But I needed to confirm my reservation. I'd have to get all the way downtown and back without being spotted. Katie wished me luck. She laughed, but it seemed very serious to me.

The dust and gravel of the road down were sensible and comforting. I loved everything that was ordinary. The ticket office hummed a lullaby of reassurance. Everything was in order and on schedule. The office and the neat lady behind the counter were both clean machines. I felt grateful. These people would get me home. Rockefeller and Ford were right after all.

I was walking back up the road, staying over to the side, in the shade, not too fast, not too slow, so as not to attract any attention. I wasn't even halfway there when I sensed a vehicle coming up behind me in a peculiar way, not quite overtaking me. I couldn't believe it could be them—just happening upon me? A red pickup pulled up alongside and then slowed down next to me. I couldn't believe this. Had they been lying in wait? Had they posted scouts, sent out spies?

Kenny was up front in the passenger seat, on my side of the road. When I looked up, he was gazing ahead, stone-faced, as though he hadn't seen me. He was wearing a clean shirt with the sleeves rolled way up on his big arms. The eyebrow I saw was at forty-five degrees—a sure sign—and his eyelids were heavy, another sign. I stopped. The truck stopped. Danny was at the wheel. He leaned forward to see past Kenny. "Where you heading, Prop?" Kenny turned, then, to look at me, and the demon in his eyes grinned. Before I could say anything, I heard Pope. He was hanging out over the side of the open back of the truck. "Come on, shit-face. Where you been? We're down to the last of the party booze. We need you to help get Marie to sell us a jug." Freeman and the Nicholson brothers were in the back too, and I saw at once that they had at least one bottle now but were just sober enough to be thinking of the future.

The handwriting was writ large on the wall. The raven had cawed three times and flown north. The crystal ball looked like the raven's eye. Mere anarchy was loosed upon the world. The jig was up.

It appeared that they had been looking for me. Danny

wanted to hear that song again, that pretty old ballad about true love reunited. Kenny wanted, after all the years of standing off suspiciously, to shake my hand, holding on to it and looking at me with soft eyes, telling me I was a hell of a guy. Louie reminded me that if you don't drink you're no good. Louie wasn't comfortable in the white man's world: It was too cold for an Eskimo. Firewater helped a lot. Jerry and Bobby hoisted me on board, Jerry looking more than ever like Alan Ladd in *This Gun for Hire*, only with black hair, and Bobby wanted to know again, "What do you think of us Asiatic throwbacks, Professor?"

Okay. But I meant to stand my ground. Pope had gotten out to take a leak behind the cover of the open door of the truck, and I looked right at him. "Okay. But if I miss that plane, I'm going to be really *pissed*."

"Don't sweat it, Professor," Pope said, white teeth gleaming. But I wouldn't let go of his eyes, and his eyes told me I had his word. "You'll be on that plane."

Okay, then, I let go. I took a good one from the jug and felt better right away. Where were we off to?

❀

It is Sunday. The bars and liquor stores are closed. But the lady who runs the hotel also runs a liquor store. Where there's hope there may be firewater. They pull up to the side of the gray clapboard hotel. The Professor, as the only one with high-tone credentials and proper English, is delegated to talk Marie into letting them have a couple of under-the-counter jugs. She is a business and money person, and they count on her lust for the dollar to overcome her religious scruples and fear of the law. Pope is to go along, wearing his best Jack Armstrong look, to add a little weight to the encounter.

Marie appears a minute or so after they enter and call sweetly, "Hi, Marie. Anybody home?" The small lobby contains a sofa and a couple of worn overstuffed armchairs, but Pope and the Professor intend to remain standing, in attendance on her presence. The Professor begins to explain to her, as one respectable person to another, what is on their minds. She is middle-aged, shapeless, and anonymous. She appears oddly agitated at the sight of them.

"Oh, no," she interrupts, her voice unaccountably rising. "Oh, no. You get right on out of here. I know all about you two. Pope and the Professor." It startles the Professor to see that she is frightened of him. Him—Professor Robert Allen Durr!? She seems on the verge of hysteria. Her voice is quavering, and the finger pointing at them is shaking. "Don't make me have to call the trooper now!"

With hasty reassurances and vague apologies for having bothered her on a Sunday, they back off and stumble over each other getting out the door. The Professor is trying to assimilate the fact that this portly commercial lady regards him somehow as a reprobate, someone, a kind of savage, who has jumped the reservation and is therefore a threat, clientele for troopers. Had he been up to more than he can remember at one or another of D Inn Crowd's celebrations?

They wind up in Arlene's apartment, of all places—a motel kind of apartment with a kitchen of convenience—as advertised. There are more brothers present, and a few bunnies have materialized, Carla and Irene and a friend of theirs brimming with interest. Arlene is busy tending to her children, but it's all right if they make use of her ice cubes. She even pauses once, when Pope is ending a song, to ask for a certain number, one Pope and the Professor do together, but otherwise she seems not to have noticed the Professor.

The jugs are passed, the songs sung, even the long ballad Danny likes, and the time is slipping away from them. When they try to catch hold of its tail it's already too far gone. The airport is a few miles out of town, the airport bus has already departed. And the red pickup truck is no longer parked outside. It had been borrowed, and its owner has driven it away. The

BOB DURR

Professor puts down the guitar deliberately and looks over at
Pope. "Let us not talk falsely now, the hour is getting late."

Pope gets up, tucks in his shirttails, and assumes his serious
and sincere look. "Have one more for the road, Professor. I'll be
right back." He hitches up his pants and starts for the door. In
the small modern apartment, his walk—elbows cocked, arms
swinging, one shoulder higher than the other, big bold strides
on a rolling deck—seems oddly exaggerated, improbable.

He reappears quickly, and triumphantly, with what looks like
an antique flivver, a rattletrap thing so dilapidated the rattles
had got away. About a dozen of D Inn Crowd and honorary
bunnies volunteer to see the Professor off. They pile into the
flivver two and three deep. Scouts sit on the fenders, and a
couple ride shotgun on the running boards. The Professor plays
guitar, with his picking arm around Irene on his lap. Everyone
joins in on the chorus of "Down in Bristol Bay." They pass
through town like an animated cartoon.

Pope is at the wheel, concentrating on getting there before
the plane takes off. His honor is at stake. Fortunately the engine
of the old jalopy isn't as tight as he is, because he has it to the
floor but is barely achieving speed limit. Turns in the road are
exciting; the old car would like to abandon the right-of-way and
head off across the tundra but lacks the wherewithal.

As they screech into the airport the twin-engine liner is
closed up and taxiing for the runway. This, however, is not Ken-
nedy. It's really just a big field with runways. Pope never hesitates or slows down. With the running board and fender riders
holding on and yelling and everyone else leaning out and waving and yelling, "Wait! Wait!" he swings out in front of the
aircraft. The plane stops, the gangplank lowers. Brothers and
bunnies tumble out of the flivver. Pope and Johanson hoist the
Professor up onto their shoulders and carry him to the waiting
airplane. Everyone has to shake his hand or give him a kiss. The
stewardess stands in the doorway smiling. P. G. happens to be

standing off a ways, watching, and he's grinning and shaking his head. P. G.'s Indians at it again.

Then the Professor is on board and seated by a window. As the plane turns he sees them all waving, and then he is up and away and all he can see is yellow water and green tundra and in the distance the mountains of Bristol Bay.

❋

Like a stone thrown into a pool, a memorable event has a ripple effect. The effect of that D Inn Crowd party rippled all the way into the domesticated skies of New York State. The stewardesses seemed to understand and commiserate with their shaky passenger; they kept bringing me scotches. At home, for a few days, Tom Collins ministered to the lingering reverberations, but then I could once more drink my coffee without the help of a towel.

It was in the following year, 1968, that I resigned my professorship, sold or gave away all my possessions, and with my family moved to the Lake Iliamna wilderness, about a mile from Gene Pope and his family.

But that, as they say in Tierra del Fuego, is another story.

I wrote the first draft of this book some twenty-five years ago, and then my life intervened and I became too preoccupied with surviving physically and psychologically to go back into it. That's a long and somewhat strange story, subject for another book. Briefly, the Bureau of Land Management kicked us off Iliamna Lake after only a year, at which point we were destitute. My family and I managed to get to Les VanDevere's setnet site at Chinitna Bay, Cook Inlet, where we wintered in 1969, and from there, in the spring of 1970, we moved to the Susitna Valley, ten roadless miles north of the town of Talkeetna, where we got a piece of land on a little lake via the state's Open to Entry program. Our cabin burned down in 1973, and shortly afterward my marriage crashed and burned. (This was not a case of cause and effect. Woods life was indeed good for family life, and Carol was a great wilderness woman. The troubles with the marriage went way back and were personal.)

But as regards this book, all those years and all that living and learning between the first draft and the final draft were to the good because I came to realize that my first go at the Bristol Bay story had missed something important, something of the essence, really. That first draft was all about the adventures and misadventures, the trials, tribulations, and comedic aspects of an

English professor who had grown up on the streets of Brooklyn trying to become an Alaskan fisherman and frontiersman. Which was well and good. That's a big part of the story, and telling it was great fun. But what I missed in that first telling, probably because I was too close to it to see it, was something pivotal in my life, something that had been brewing for many years—decades, even—before I went to Alaska and Bristol Bay, something the realization of which is now pervasive in the book. The underlying adventure, the crucial endeavor was my inchoate thrust to break the mind-forged manacles that had kept me chained to the specious reality conjured up by a mad civilization. What I wanted in Bristol Bay was more than proving up as a fisherman so I could support my family in the woods. What I wanted was a breakthrough to primal sanity. I was after my birthright in the real world. Pope and P. G's Indians and all that firewater and mayhem and the whisperings of the wild land and the wild sea were the initial outrageous and paradoxical shock therapy necessary to break me loose in ways other than intellectual. I already had the philosophy; I needed to have it proved upon my pulses.

And now after thirty years I still live in the woods, on this little lake in this log cabin I and my family and friends built: every year deeper into the woods. If I weren't here already I would be doing everything I could to get here.

In Bristol Bay it was "the Professor." Around Talkeetna for the past twenty-eight years it's been "Jungle Bob."

Gene Pope is alive and well, living with his family in Intricate Bay on Iliamna Lake, and we are still friends.